FIRST LESSONS

A Report on Elementary Education in America

by William J. Bennett
U.S. Secretary of Education
September 1986

TABLE OF CONTENTS

INTRODUCTION:

THE YEAR OF THE ELEMENTARY SCHOOL

Within the next decade, almost 50 million children will pass through the doors of America's elementary schools.[1] This year alone, in 80,000 elementary schools across the United States, 31 million boys and girls will be taught by 1.45 million teachers.[2] By the middle of the 1990's, enrollments will nearly equal those of the "baby boom" years following World War II.

Elementary education is an enterprise of vast proportions in this nation; and for each child it is an experience of unsurpassed importance. After the family, elementary school is the most influential institution in children's lives: helping to shape first and lasting views of themselves, molding aspirations and skills, introducing them to their country, their culture, to the universe itself.

Yet since 1953, no major national report has examined the condition of elementary education.[3] The "excellence movement" of recent years has looked closely at our high schools and, to a lesser extent, our colleges. But it has not yet paid sustained attention to the condition of elementary education. The time has come to do so—not because elementary schools are in deep trouble, but because they are so deeply important.

After studying elementary schools, visiting them, discussing them, and consulting with some of the country's leading educators, I conclude that American elementary education is not menaced by a "rising tide of mediocrity." It is, overall, in pretty good shape. By some measures, elementary schools are doing better now than they have in years. Yet elementary education in the United States could be better still. Indeed, it will need to be better in the years ahead because we depend so much on it, because not all schools are yet as good as they ought to be—and because it is not in our nature as a society to settle for less than excellence for all.

In the remainder of this report I go into some detail about the condition and direction of elementary education in America. Let me here set forth certain general observations and recommendations:

1) The principal goals of elementary education are to build for every child a

1

strong foundation for further education, for democratic citizenship, and for eventual entry into responsible adulthood.

2) Parents have the central role in children's education and must be empowered to play it successfully.

3) Children do not just "grow up." They must be **raised** by the community of adults—all adults. The community should accept as its solemn responsibility—as a covenant—the nurture, care, and education of the coming generation.

4) Teachers should be enabled to become professionals. Certification should depend on demonstrated knowledge and skills, not on paper credentials.

5) The principalship should be deregulated so that accomplished people from many fields may become elementary school principals.

6) In order to provide for more teaching and more learning, elementary schools will need more learning time.

7) The chronological lockstep by which children ordinarily enter and progress through school should be loosened to provide for differences in children's abilities.

8) In specific curriculum areas:
   - Every elementary school can and must teach all its students to read.

   - Children should learn that writing is more than filling in blanks. Writing must be part of the whole curriculum, not just language arts.

   - Elementary schools need to teach science, and their science programs should include "hands-on," experimental activities in addition to texts and lectures.

   - Mathematics should extend beyond simple computation and should emphasize problem solving.

   - The social studies curriculum should be transformed. Schools should teach children not only the basic lessons and habits of life in democratic societies, but also impart to them substantial instruction in history, geography, and civics, beginning at the earliest ages.

   - The arts and instruction in the arts should be integral parts of every elementary school.

   - Children should gain a basic grasp of the uses and limitations of computers.

   - Elementary curricula should include health and physical education.

   - Every school should have a library, and every child should have and use a public library card.

First Things First

What should a child know?

In an address at the National Press Club, shortly after becoming Secretary of Education, thinking mainly about high schools, I tried to answer that question as follows:

> We should want every student to know how mountains are made, and that for most actions there is an equal and opposite reaction. They should know who said 'I am the state' and who said 'I have a dream.' They should know about subjects and predicates, about isosceles triangles and ellipses. They should know where the Amazon flows and what the First Amendment means. They should know about the Donner Party and slavery, and Shylock, Hercules, and Abigail Adams, where Ethiopia is, and why there is a Berlin Wall....[4]

I refer back to this litany because in our examination of elementary education we asked much the same question and received a closely related answer. While we do not expect sixth-graders to understand the geopolitical implications of the Berlin Wall, we hope that they can locate the divided city on a map. While elementary graduates cannot be expected to give a sophisticated analysis of the slavery issue, we can reasonably believe that they will have heard about Dred Scott, and will know that slavery was a major cause of the Civil War.

In other words, we may plausibly expect that elementary school will give our children the basic facts and understandings of our civilization, and that it will equip them with the skills to apprehend more complex knowledge, thus awakening the appetite for further learning.

Since elementary education is so large a subject, in tackling it I have had to make some fundamental choices. Accordingly, this report will not treat separately each segment or interest within elementary education. You will not find one section on rural schools and another on urban, or a unit each on private, parochial, and public schools. This report is about elementary education as a whole. It concerns itself not with the geographic or economic differences that set one kind of school apart from others, but with the characteristics, habits, curricula, and spirit that typify the best schools in any geographic or socioeconomic setting. You will not find a price tag attached to this report, either—though you will hear a call for communities to commit the necessary resources. The most serious problems facing our elementary schools do not derive from a lack of money; they derive from a surfeit of confusion, bureaucratic thinking, and community apathy. Simply throwing more funds at these problems is no solution. The improvement of elementary schools requires fresh approaches, better incentives, and inventive leadership.

In the United States, elementary schools come in many configurations: kindergarten through sixth; K-3; 4-6; K-8; and so on. For the purpose of this report, let us think in terms of two basic definitions: First, elementary **education** is everything that children learn, for good or for ill, before reaching adolescence. It includes not only formal schooling but also the combined influences of home, family, neighborhood, peers, and media. Second, within that context, elementary **school** will be used to mean kindergarten through eighth grade. Although I touch briefly on preschool issues, I do so in the context of parents. Passages referring to "elementary school" will relate to things happening from kindergarten on.

The Year of the Elementary School

This report is one result of a larger undertaking announced in October 1985, when I suggested that the 1985-6 school year be The Year of The Elementary School. During this year, I have asked my colleagues in the Department of Education and educators across the nation to seek out, examine, and celebrate excellence in elementary education.

In 1985-86, the Department's School Recognition Program, which previously was focused exclusively on secondary schools, was redirected to elementary schools. Later this month, a ceremony here in Washington will honor 270 high-achieving elementary schools from across the United States.

Last year I also visited a score of elementary schools in as many communities. There I had occasion not only to meet talented teachers and extraordinary principals but also to teach and talk with young students. I tried my hand at teaching history to these youngsters, and found the experience challenging, rewarding, and encouraging.

In October 1985, I named an Elementary Education Study Group, comprised of 21 distinguished Americans. I asked them to assist me in the preparation of this report. In four public meetings, numerous papers and letters, and any number of conversations, they have proved invaluable partners. In reading this report, you will from time to time come across explicit mention of their contributions—but the entirety of the work has benefited from their probing inquiry and trenchant analyses. I am deeply grateful for their generosity, their enthusiasm, their insight. I should add, however, that although members of the Study Group contributed immeasurably to this report, and had an opportunity to review it in draft form, responsibility for its content is mine. The report has been informed not only by Study Group deliberations, but also by extensive staff research, by studies undertaken by public and private organizations around the country, and by correspondence from interested individuals and groups. The final product, set forth in the pages that follow, reflects my own distillation of these sources, my own judgments and conclusions. This report is not a statement of federal policy; it is a statement of my views on matters principally the business of state, local, and private authorities to decide. Whether any school, school board, parent organization, or teachers' group wishes to implement the views and recommendations contained in these pages is its decision to make.

Though the current movement for education reform has largely skipped the elementary grades, past decades have seen numerous reports and studies concerning the goals and practices of American elementary education. The earliest of these we have seen is an 1895 report by the National Educational (sic) Association's Committee of Fifteen, which in three separate documents examined the training of teachers, the organization of city school systems, and the "correlation of studies," or curricular content of elementary school. The subcommittee that wrote this third report was chaired by U. S. Commissioner of Education William T. Harris.

Other studies of elementary education included a subsequent National Education Association report in 1922; a 1927 report of the Commonwealth Fund's Commission on Length of Elementary Education; another NEA report, entitled "Education for All American Children," issued in 1948; a 1952 survey by the U.S. Office of Education called "Schools at Work in 48 States;" and a 1953 review of "Elementary School Objectives" by the Russell Sage Foundation.

Many issues addressed in these earlier works resemble those dealt with in this report, and so from time to time I have inserted into the text a brief passage from one of these predecessor documents.* While these excerpts do not necessarily reflect the overall tenor of each prior report, I believe the reader will be struck by the continuity of concerns, sometimes even the similarity of language in which those concerns have been addressed, from generation to generation.

I trust that *First Lessons* is a worthy successor to these reports going back almost a century. It is not intended only for educators. Much of what follows may already be well known to teachers and principals. My aim is to extend an understanding of elementary education beyond the schoolhouse door, into the homes of students and their parents; into meetings of school boards, into offices of legislators, into executive suites of our business and financial institutions. I want American communities to understand the central importance of elementary education and to overcome the misguided notion, so evident in the distribution of our attention and resources, that it is somehow less important than secondary or higher education. Education is a continuum, lasting a lifetime. Elementary education is its critical beginning.

---

*In the text, the passages will be identified by date as follows: 1895 – The Report of the National Educational Association's Committee of Fifteen; 1948 – Education for All American Children, *National Education Association;* 1953 – Elementary School Objectives, *The Russell Sage Foundation.*

CHAPTER I:

CHILDREN, PARENTS, AND THE COMMUNITY OF ADULTS

Children

The most important fact about those who attend elementary school is that they are children. Unlike high school and college students, elementary school pupils are still navigating the high seas of early development, exploring a new world of information, and seeking to master their own minds and bodies in the process. Young children are full of contradictions. They are stubborn and malleable; persistent and distracted; charming and incorrigible. So, in discussing educational practices and policies that will affect them, let us begin by stipulating their uniqueness.

Let us begin, also, with the recognition that the world of children is not so simple. From the day they are born, today's children are plunged into an environment that goes well beyond the boundaries of family, school, neighborhood, and town. At the age of 5 or 6, today's child may already have heard more music, seen more artistic images, and witnessed more real or televised violence than a child born in 1800 would likely have encountered in a lifetime.

Our elementary schools, then, have plenty to cope with. Moreover, in the population of children about to arrive, our schools face unprecedented challenges. Annual elementary enrollments will reach 35 million by the early 90s,[1] and this will be a crowd of children like never before, reflecting at least three remarkable infusions of diversity within our population.

First, we are racially and ethnically heterogeneous. We have always been a nation of immigrants, drawing individuals and families who flee poverty, oppression, and despair elsewhere on the planet to knock upon our "golden door." We continue to welcome newcomers to our shores, knowing that there are no more solid citizens, no more enterprising and productive workers, no more enthusiastic Americans than those who come here by choice and who still remember what it is like elsewhere.

Today's immigrant and refugee tide is more varied than ever before. It is less European than in the past. It consists of a greater diversity of hues and languages, of religions and beliefs, of cultural habits and mores. All this makes for added   7 challenges—but they are challenges we embrace. There is no more exhilarating sight in American education today than a second or fifth grade class comprised of 25 children from almost as many lands—but all learning together, in common, the skills and knowledge that will enable them to become productive adults and responsible citizens.

Second, our diversity is socioeconomic. We are rich and we are poor and most of us are somewhere in between. Yet the persistence of a socioeconomic "underclass" in American society looms as one of the largest challenges to our nation in general and to our education system in particular. Lack of money is only one aspect of the problem, and perhaps not even the most serious. Dependency, crime, ill health, joblessness, drug addiction—these are not, of course, confined to the poor, nor do most low income individuals experience them. But when they intersect within that knot of poverty that sociologists often refer to as the "underclass," we have an authentic and sizable problem for which the term "diversity" is not nearly expressive enough—a challenge increasingly troubling our elementary schools.

Third, we face large changes in the structure of the families in which our children are raised.* To recount some sobering demographic facts, we can borrow Harold Hodgkinson's description of the family circumstances of a randomly-selected 100 children born in 1986—the kindergarten class of 1991. Of these 100 youngsters, 12 have been born to unmarried parents; 40 have been born to parents who will divorce before the child is 18 years old; 5 have parents who will separate; 2 have been born to parents at least one of whom will die during the child's first 18 years. Only 41 of these 100 boys and girls will reach their 18th birthdays in "traditional" family units.[2]

These are formidable changes. Yet for two centuries, our schools have reveled in diversity, and have served to bind rich and poor, Yankee and immigrant, with the threads of democratic experience. In this report, I acknowledge these changes as reality—but do not take them to be insuperable obstacles. Because we know that all children can learn, and because we understand that educational excellence can transcend barriers of race, ethnicity, and income, this report will concentrate on issues fundamental to learning: What should children know? How can they learn it?

To begin answering those questions, we naturally turn to children's first and most influential teachers: their parents.

Parents

Parents belong at the center of a young child's education. The single best way to improve elementary education is to strengthen parents' role in it, both by reinforc-

---

*I look forward to the forthcoming White House report on the family— directed by Under Secretary of Education Gary L. Bauer—and to a companion study on welfare. Both are issues of considerable importance for elementary education and deserve fuller examination than is possible in these pages.

ing their relationship with the school and by helping and encouraging them in their own critical job of teaching the young. Not all teachers are parents, but all parents are teachers.

Parents' oversight of their children's education ought not be limited to the margins. We already expect parents to make a wide array of choices: whether to start a child in preschool or kindergarten; whether to accept or contest a recommendation for retention, and so on. We expect—and should expect—parents to engage themselves directly in their children's education: to read to them if they can, to ask others to read to them if they cannot, to encourage children to read on their own, to meet with teachers, to ensure that homework gets done, to furnish necessary supplies and materials, perhaps above all to convey to their children—not just once, but incessantly—the immense value that they, the parents, assign to a good education.

It is reasonable that parents be accountable for how well they fulfill these obligations. At the same time, however, parents need to be able to hold a school accountable for what it does with and for and to their children. This is commonplace within private education, where children attend schools chosen by their parents. What is less widely recognized is that within the framework of public education, many parents also choose the schools their children attend: by deciding to live in particular towns or neighborhoods, by lining up at dawn to enroll their youngster in a special school within the local system, by obtaining a variety of waivers and permissions to enable their child to attend a school other than the one to which he would ordinarily be assigned. It is also a fact that many public school systems now intentionally furnish parents with choices by diversifying educational offerings and organizing "magnet" schools providing various curricular enticements.

For example, the brochure for St. Nicholas Avenue Classical Learning Center, a public elementary school in Worcester, Massachusetts, asserts: "All children need to be challenged by an expanded curriculum.... All children need the opportunity to experiment, discover, collect, explore, learn and grow in their academic environment." Another Worcester public "magnet" school, Columbus Park Preparatory Academy, proclaims that it "will emphasize discipline and order and will expect a high level of self-control and responsibility on the part of each student...." Within Worcester's public schools, parents can decide which emphasis is correct for their children.

When teachers and principals know that parents have voluntarily chosen their school, a new dynamic is created for learning. Says Study Group member Charles Glenn: "We have come to believe that a system of parent choice among schools, if properly organized by an aggressive central administration, can release the energies which only diversity makes available, without sacrificing accountability for the effective education of every child."

In New York's Central Harlem District 5, Superintendent Luther Seabrook has ordered the end of "zoning" (the assignment of students to neighborhood schools) and has told principals that they must compete for the district's 11,800 students by offering a variety of specialized programs. Since the program's inception in 1982, reading scores have climbed, and more than 1,000 new students have moved into the system from private schools and adjoining districts.[3]

I propose that we acknowledge parents' right to choose their children's schools as the norm, not the exception, and that we extend it to as many parents as possible— not just to those fortunate enough to live in particular communities or wealthy enough to change their place of residence. The child, the Supreme Court made clear in *Pierce v. Society of Sisters* (1925), "is not the mere creature of the state." Today more than ever we need to empower parents with respect to the education of their children. This must include affording them an array of alternatives—and holding them accountable for choosing wisely. For the larger community of adults—here ordinarily acting through state or local government—has some rights and responsibilities, too. Parents are not free to deny their children an education that will meet certain basic standards set by the larger society. Children are not the property of the state, but neither are they the property of their parents. They are not property at all.

While asserting parents' primacy in education, we cannot treat the word "family" as a magical incantation. The family does not always work as well as it should. In fact, in the words of Study Group member Lois Coit, "schools must address the issue of parents who are failing their children." Changes in family structure and behavior are having a profound impact on elementary schools.

Half of today's marriages end in divorce.[4] The proportion of children being raised in one-parent homes is rising. And the children of unwed teenagers are creating a new "baby boom" in precisely the economic stratum least able to afford it. In light of these facts, we cannot simply suppose that reliance on the family will cure all the ills of education.

Another change, very different in nature, involves the emergence of women as full participants in the labor market. Seventy percent of mothers with children 6 to 13 years old are now in the labor force.[5] Over half of married women with children under 6 have outside employment.[6] When both parents work, or when a single working parent—mother or father—is raising a child alone, it often means that schools, other adults, and community institutions bear a correspondingly larger share of the responsibility for children.

Income does not determine the quality of parenting. Rich and poor alike can exert profound effects on children's education. These may be positive or negative. Some affluent families meet all their children's needs—even spoil them with costly things—but fail to meet their subtler educational, emotional, and moral needs. A mother raising three children in the poorest part of town may be able to instill more effectively in her children a sense that she cares about their education, and that scholastic achievement is important.

Neither does family structure guarantee parental excellence. The traditional nuclear family is the paradigm and the basis for much of our social organization; yet two neglectful parents are of less use to children than one who is attentive and

10

caring. I want to be clear: Nothing in this report should be construed as criticism of single parents who are conscientious in their duties. I know whereof I speak. My brother and I were raised by a single parent, and we owe her the deepest thanks and praise. My mother understood, however, and I came to learn from her, that single parenthood is more difficult than parenthood shared with a partner. Raising children alone is a hard job.

The primary requisites for parental cooperation in the enterprise of education, for two parents or one, are attitude and commitment. As Ken Levine, a Baltimore mathematics teacher, wrote, "Children coming from a home where one or both parents come to school, meet the teacher, and know the curriculum, come from a home with a message: 'We value what you do. Your success is important to us'....And children coming from a home where the parents do not get involved get an equally clear message: 'You're on your own. Let us know how things work out.' "[7] Some people contend that we cannot expect much from parents who lack education, money, or a solid grasp of the English language. Yet for generations, our schools have successfully taught the children of immigrants and refugees who insisted on making the fearful trip to meet the teacher because they knew school was important; the children of working-class people who did not know how to read very well but who made sure that their children completed their lessons each night; and the children of the poor, hopeful that their families could escape poverty by learning. Today, millions of low-income and ill-educated parents do their utmost to further their children's education. Saying that poor parents cannot be expected to help because they are poor is snobbism of the worst sort, and it is wrong.

When parents need assistance, they should find that other members of the adult community are ready to extend it. Since we know, for example, that reading to young children helps them learn to read, illiterate parents should have sources of help with this activity. Each community can find suitable ways of providing such assistance: Parents certainly are not the only possible "readers." Many libraries organize excellent story hours, sometimes staffed by librarians, sometimes by senior citizens, sometimes by regular volunteers. Cousins, uncles, and neighbors can read aloud to other people's children. And there is no reason a local radio station cannot produce and broadcast a story hour several evenings a week.

Reading, of course, is just one of parents' many jobs. They may need other kinds of assistance or advice. The State of Missouri has inaugurated a "Parents as First Teachers" program which provides parents of children under three with information about child development, access to screening and health programs, and periodic visits with educators and other parents. (First results of a pilot study were impressive: In tests of mental acuity, children whose parents took part in the program scored significantly higher than control groups.) Whatever the issue at hand, the community should be there to provide help for parents who really need it.

Parents and Schools: A Reciprocal Relationship

Once a child is enrolled in elementary school, parents and school need to develop reciprocal relations. Parents have a right to expect high standards and sound practices, and schools should be able to depend on parents to hold up their end of the instructional bargain. Today, elementary school teachers often complain that children start school lacking certain basic social skills. It is reasonable to ask that when first graders get to school, they should know not to interrupt; should know "excuse me," "please," "thank-you," and the other signals by which we negotiate the rapids of social interaction. I am not just invoking Miss Manners here; children's ability to learn in school may actually depend in part upon their mastery of these skills.

> *At this stage the standards of politeness, of honesty, of correct or moral behavior that are shown by children, especially in any situation that is encountered for the first time in school, are largely the result of family and home environment.* —1953

Remember, also, that these are the first lessons of living in a democracy. We take turns; we follow and lead; we solve disputes by appeal to reason, not fists; we help others when they are in danger; we stand up for what's right. These simple lessons learned in home and school resonate through the great decisions of our national life.

Reciprocity between parents and school implies a significant commitment on parents' part. Here are some specific parental practices that may help a child's progress:

- Establishing a quiet place where children can read and do homework; giving assistance when needed; looking over homework, helping with it when necessary, but encouraging children to manage it on their own;

- Setting limits on play time and television watching;

- Staying in touch with the teacher; meeting with the teacher several times a year to examine the child's problems and successes in school;

- Checking report cards, talking with the child about problems and progress in various subjects; commenting on the child's work, providing positive reinforcement for good work;

- Taking part in PTA and school board meetings; chaperoning school trips; perhaps volunteering in the school itself.

Some parents may think they do not have the time for these very traditional activities. But parents who excuse themselves on such grounds as needing "quiet time of their own" must realize that these things **should be done** if a child's education is to be successful. They are the kinds of steps that can be taken by all parents, regardless of educational background—and they come with the territory of parenthood.

12   Because of cultural differences, distance, or other factors, some interested parents

remain reluctant to get involved—and some school districts are finding creative solutions. When parents from the San Carlos Apache Reservation in eastern Arizona could not get to school meetings, the local district provided transportation and babysitting services, and attendance improved. When three districts in New Hampshire's White Mountain region needed to get parents and teachers of handicapped children to cooperate more closely, they jointly developed "communication books." These are notebooks carried by the student between home and school, and allow parents and teachers to "talk" on a daily basis about the child's problems and growth.[8]

Parents' own beliefs also influence their children's most basic attitudes about schoolwork. Harold Stevenson's comparative studies have found, for example, that American mothers tend to believe ability determines a child's performance in school, while Japanese mothers tend to ascribe success to effort.[9] Isn't the latter value system more likely to produce hard work than one which holds success to be the product of innate gifts or mere chance?

> *The chief consideration...is this requirement of the civilization into which the child is born, as determining not only what he shall study in school, but what habits and customs he shall be taught in the family before the school age arrives....* —1895

Then there is the matter of values *per se*. No one can teach these better than parents can exemplify them. Although most teachers seek to reinforce good character in their students by teaching honesty, industry, loyalty, self-respect, and other virtues, their presentation of certain issues may yet be clouded by foolish "value-free" education theories—and by their perception of conflicts among value systems represented in their students' diverse backgrounds. Some teachers fear that controversy may ensue if they tackle moral issues too directly. This all makes it doubly important that parents provide sound moral education in the home. Parents can and should discuss ethical, religious, and spiritual concerns which children might not hear addressed elsewhere.

What is to be done when the reciprocal obligations of parents and school are not being satisfactorily fulfilled? The parent who feels the school is not doing its part has several modes of recourse: from calling on the teacher all the way to transferring the child to another school. The school, in turn, should be able to call problems to parents' attention. Hence schools should consider reserving a corner of the child's report card in which to suggest how parents might better fulfill their responsibilities as partners in the educational process.

Parents and The Popular Culture

It has always been a prime responsibility of parents to mediate for their children between the serious matters that need to be learned and the beguiling distractions of entertainment and play. A challenge facing today's parents is that electronic media have brought the outside world into the home, making it more difficult to guide children's attention.

The average child between 6 and 11 years of age spends 25 hours per week — roughly one third of non-school hours — watching television.[10] Says Yale University's Dr. Victor Strasburger: "By the time they graduate from high school, children will have spent 15,000 hours camped in front of a TV set.... During this time, they will have witnessed some 18,000 murders and countless robberies, bombings, smugglings, assaults, beatings and tortures. They will have been exposed to some 350,000 commercial messages...."[11]

Let us face this one squarely. If Americans did not care about our future, we might let the next generation turn into listless watchers. But at the same time as adults across America are avidly discussing education reform, and working to compete more successfully in the world, we are allowing too many of our children to spend their days and nights slack-jawed before the tube.

The media are capable of helping. Television can inform and enlighten; consider the thoughtful ABC biography of Theodore Roosevelt or the PBS series on Beatrix Potter. But, all too often, unsupervised children spin the dial to programs they hardly benefit from watching.

Nor is the selection of programs the only problem. We must reckon as well with the "passive" nature of television itself. Parents and teachers can help by prodding youngsters to question and discuss what they see. We should do much more of this. But let us not be timid about curbing television time itself.

The record of research is clear: Excessive television viewing can hurt youngsters' school achievement. We also know that nonstop viewing is particularly damaging to children of above-average intelligence. With too much TV, we may be doing disproportionate damage to the best minds of the younger generation.

Children need quiet time, time to explore their thoughts as well as their physical surroundings. A home saturated by electronic media cannot provide the cerebral space a child's intellectual development demands. *Time* essayist Lance Morrow has captured a puzzle of our age: "The great intellectual flowering of New England in the 19th century ... resulted in part from the very thinness of the New England atmosphere, an understimulation that made introspection a sort of cultural resource. America today is so chaotically hyped, its air so thick with kinetic information and alarming images and television and drugs, that the steady gaze required for excellence is nearly impossible."[12]

It is the responsibility of parents to set limits on their children's television viewing, to monitor and discuss the content of what they do watch, and to set a good example for their children by restraining their own TV viewing.

Of course, "pop culture" is more than television. I grew up with rock and roll — and still like it. But some of today's rock stars sing to children in terms that would shock a sailor. Eight-year-olds are hearing about matters best left to psychoanalysis or the confessional. People who call parents' attention to this trend shouldn't be thought of as bluenoses or censors. It is not prudery to be alarmed by assaults on the sensibilities of the young.

14

It seems to me that radio, despite some ill-conceived programming, retains a great and largely untapped potential. It can make intellectual demands and stimulate the imagination in ways TV cannot. Some stations have taken commendable steps toward the reestablishment of radio as a positive force in children's lives. Every weeknight, for example, New York's WNYC originates "Kids America," a magazine-style show now being broadcast for children 6 to 12 years old in 14 cities around the United States. And National Public Radio deserves plaudits for "Children's Radio Theatre." Let us hope these initial efforts will inspire large-scale ventures from the commercial radio networks.

Popular culture transcends the limitations of mass media. Communities across America offer parents the opportunity to introduce their children to live theater, classical music, ballet, and art exhibitions. A child doesn't need Broadway or the Los Angeles Philharmonic to appreciate the performing arts. Community theaters, university chamber ensembles and amateur dance companies have given millions of young people their first exhilarating glimpse of the treasures of our culture.

The Community of Adults

Parents are the central figures, captains of the vessel on which children voyage to maturity. But they are not the entire crew. Even as a ship captain must be able to rely on expert navigators, engine-room technicians, and cargo handlers, so must parents be able to draw on the expertise, the caring, the energies, the support, the example of other adults: of family members, neighbors, church members, friends, teachers, doctors, policemen, television writers, social workers, advertisers, clergy, legislators, professors, and coaches. What is more, when parents are absent, inept or irresponsible, though it is folly to suppose that others can truly replace them, it is nevertheless imperative that the community of adults do all within its power to fill in for them. It matters not whether the child is rich or poor, black or white, brilliant or slow. Children who tomorrow will join the community of adults should be the foremost concern of that community today.

Though only 27 percent of American households include school-age children,[13] we cannot afford to regard elementary education as the exclusive concern of parents and professional educators. If our institutions, values, and knowledge are to make it into the next century in good shape, we must come to regard the education of young children as a task shared by all adults. We must see it as a **covenant** with the family firmly at its center; with the adult community supporting—not supplanting—the family; and with elementary schools as a fundamental expression of the community's values and aspirations.

> *The School belongs to all of the community, not just to those who have children in it. The American public school is a school of all the people.*
>
> *—1948*

When we form this covenant, what is the task to which we mutually agree? What, in other words, is the **goal** of American elementary education? I believe its highest   15 purposes are to prepare children well for further education and to lay the ground-work for their own eventual entry into the community of responsible adults and democratic citizens. In our time, in this land, democratic citizenship requires an array of knowledge and skills: a common language through which we all can communicate; an understanding of our civilization and its institutions; knowledge of our national symbols; a grasp of America's unique cultural pluralism; and respect for the values and precepts that enable people from different backgrounds to live together as Americans.

The specific purpose of schools within this covenant is to provide a foundation – to teach the grammar and syntax through which our many American voices speak to one another. This means, of course, the basic skills of reading, writing, and math. But it also means historical, scientific, geographic, and civic literacy; it means art and music, and all the tools with which our children can build lives of independence, virtue, and wisdom.

Since elementary schools are virtually the only institution in our society in which attendance is compulsory for everyone, we have asked them to perform all sorts of functions unrelated to their instructional mission. Study Group member Leanna Landsmann writes: "Our schools are asked to do a lot more than they can, and rather than say 'no,' schools try. They are considered the tool to achieve widespread integration, to teach children health, to feed the hungry, to help counsel children of divorce. Now it's time to encourage supportive partnerships that relieve schools of noninstructional services."

Schools do not exist in a vacuum. They are institutions consciously established by the adult community to transmit its norms, its experience, its values, and its knowledge. To pluck elementary schools out of their setting is to ignore the way our children actually live. By the end of eighth grade, as Study Group member Allan Shedlin points out, a child has typically spent 9,000 hours in school – but 95,000 hours outside of school. The home, the family, the neighborhood, the television set rival the impact of school on that child's development. So long as we view education as something that happens between 8:30 and 2:20 inside the doors of a big red brick building, we lose sight of the basic truth that "elementary education" is more than "elementary school."

Consider, for example, the education taking place for millions of American youngsters in the hours after school and before dinner. According to a 1983 study supported by the U.S. Department of Education, approximately 6 million boys and girls under age 13 routinely spend part of the day taking care of themselves.[14] These "latchkey" children are not just children of the streets, or children of working single mothers who can't afford after-school care. Many of them live with two parents in affluent suburbs. Yet when they leave school in the afternoon, they return to an empty house, or hang around on the street unattended. The principal of one suburban elementary school visited by members of the Study Group said that as many as one-third of his students were latchkey children.

It's not just the safety of these girls and boys that is in question. It's the dead time they encounter. It's all that sitting in front of the television set for lack of other stimulation. (One member of the Study Group observed that school children are fast becoming the main audience for afternoon soap operas.) It's the fact that the child who got a gold star in spelling that day comes home to a house where there is no one to tell about it. Most poignant, it's the child's own fear. *Sprint* Magazine asked its grade-school readers to write letters about how they coped with a scary situation; out of about 7,000 letters received, 5,000 dealt with the fear of being home alone, mostly after school while parents were working.[15]

The phenomenon of latchkey children is an illustration of why we need to deepen our sense of engagement with children's education. There is no question that parents are responsible for their children—before, during, and after school. But when parents cannot be home in the afternoons, they should be able to turn to other adults for help. Radio talk shows and latchkey hotlines are not enough. Better solutions can be found. In plenty of instances, parents have banded together to create child-care arrangements in their own homes or through community institutions such as the YMCA. Employers should also understand their own influence on the welfare of children, and look for ways to help their employees solve the dilemma of after-school care.

There is a tendency in contemporary American society to suppose that all educational needs of children will be met either by their parents or by government. But this ought not be assumed. The kinds of educational needs I am describing are the kinds that parents—even good parents— may need some help in meeting. And the ways in which they are best met hinge on highly individualized, flexible arrangements that government is rarely capable of making. For children, the gentle but firm counsel of elderly neighbors, the encouragement of coaches, the good example of police officers, the attention and smile of a waitress, a bus driver— all can help. In their absence, the world can become a place of alienation and fear.

The community of adults also includes myriad private associations, organizations, firms, and institutions that can assist with the education of the young. Churches are obvious and important sources of such help and already provide a great deal of it—a fact which Study Group member Edgar Nease says ought to be more generally recognized. The church or synagogue congregation is a community of adults in its own right, and these communities are especially effective in matters that bear on character formation, spiritual development, moral and ethical education. For many children the lessons of church and synagogue are profoundly influential.

Service clubs, fraternal groups, senior citizens' associations—all can enrich the education of young children and thereby strengthen the larger community. So can hospitals and medical organizations, professional societies, universities, corporations and business groups, neighborhood associations, and civic organizations. The list is lengthy and diverse in every community. Tocqueville wrote about us in the nineteenth century: "I have often admired the extreme skill with which the inhabitants of the United States succeed in proposing a common object to the exertions of a great many men and in getting them voluntarily to pursue it."[16] Whatever our walk

17

of life, the strengthening of elementary education for every youngster should be our "common object."

> *In the final analysis, the schools belong to the people. Within constitutional limits the people may, through their boards of education and state legislatures, direct the work of their schools as they will.* —1953

Consider one model for community involvement from a source that may strike some readers as unlikely: the military. After all, military bases are "neighborhoods" and have a tradition of taking care of their own. The U.S. Air Force is now opening "Family Support Centers" on each base in order to provide help for all sorts of needs. Air Force families, whatever their configuration, will be able to receive support and counseling on financial management problems, child care, and personal crises. Other communities might consider an "Office for Children," like that in Fairfax County, Virginia, which provides technical assistance to any individual or agency, public or private, that takes care of children.

The covenant of education takes many forms, and each community will interpret it in its own fashion. What must be universally acknowledged is that we are all parties to the nurture and education of young children. If we accept that, how can we shrink from doing all it implies?

CHAPTER II:

OUR ELEMENTARY SCHOOLS: "THEY TEACH US WONDERFUL THINGS!"

Once a week, a child at Frye Elementary in Chandler, Arizona, goes to the principal's office. It's not punishment; it's lunch. Principal Ray Polvani tries to get the whole school on his team—from involving a group of teachers in each year's strategic planning and managerial decisions, to having lunch each week with a student who has earned the treat. At Frye, the teachers' aides wear bright yellow T-shirts, and the walls are festooned with children's drawings and compositions. It is a place where everyone is involved in the enterprise of learning.

*   *   *   *

St. Matthew's School in Dorchester, Massachusetts, is run on a financial shoestring. But what the school lacks in money, it makes up in spirit. The classes are orderly but full of energy. A researcher might say the school has an "ethos of excellence;" Study Group member John Curnutte, after a visit, said the school's loving environment is like "a gentle magnetic compass pointing due north." The children are 98 percent Haitian—yet, while continuing to celebrate their native culture, they are learning in English rather than in French or Creole.

A visitor asks one of the children why he likes his school so much. He replies: "Because they teach us wonderful things!"

Tolstoy wrote that "all happy families are alike." In a sense, all good elementary schools are alike, too. Their goals are clearly stated and forcefully pursued by principal and staff. Their teachers find opportunities for professional development, and the act of instruction transcends method. Parents are involved. The school enjoys community support. Good schools know what to teach and how to teach—and by keeping sharply focused on their instructional mission, they can truly teach well.

We have many such elementary schools in the United States today, schools that are clear about their goals, focused in their educational aims, and well-organized in their means of achieving those aims. That is one reason the Congressional Budget Office recently was able to say: "[A]chievement in the elementary grades is now by some measures at its highest level in three decades."[1] The National Assessment of Educational Progress (NAEP) found that students at ages 9 and 13 "were better readers in 1984 than students at the same ages were in 1971."[2] And the Second International Science Study said American fifth-graders did "significantly better" in 1983 than in 1970.[3]

Looking at these results, one is tempted to say that in our elementary schools there is a rising tide of excellence. Yet such a judgment would be unwarranted: Below the surface is an undertow which ought to concern us. Writing in *The Public Interest*, analyst Barbara Lerner notes that "there was no decline in achievement in the first half of elementary school in the 1960s or in the 1970s." Yet she finds a falloff in student achievement beginning around the fifth grade and asserts that by the eighth grade "it seems comparable in magnitude to the declines at the high school level."[4]

American children do seem to be getting better at basic skills— reading, writing, and computation. Yet when asked to begin applying these skills to the acquisition of more complex knowledge, usually around fourth grade, many begin to falter. In a number of curriculum areas, international comparisons have found students in our later elementary grades failing to hold their own against students in other countries.

These outcomes suggest that from the earliest grades, our elementary schools should be doing more: not just teaching children how to add and subtract, how to write the alphabet and fill in worksheets, but also encouraging them to solve problems, to think critically, to acquire knowledge, and to organize disparate kinds of information.

To understand the essential elements of excellence in elementary school, let us turn next to what should be taught and learned there, to both the explicit and the implicit (or "hidden") curriculum.

The Explicit Curriculum

We must decide, in the words of Study Group member Don Thomas, "What is the common body of knowledge important for **all** students?" What should children know by the time they leave eighth grade?

Grammar, literature, arithmetic, geography, and history are the five branches upon which the disciplinary work of the elementary school is concentrated. —1895

In an address before the American Association for the Advancement of Science almost 50 years ago, Walter Lippmann declared that by vacating a curriculum grounded in the classical culture of the Western world, American schools and colleges were depriving citizens of their cultural traditions and contributing to the decline of Western civilization. We must still ask Lippmann's question: If our education system embraces "no common faith, no common body of principle, no common body of knowledge, no common moral and intellectual discipline....," how are we to create a civil nation? How are we to nurture democratic citizenship?[5]

20   Without a well-defined set of curricular goals, all else is superfluous. Schools

must have standards; this is as true for elementary schools as for colleges and high schools. It is imperative that elementary educators focus first on the acquisition of basic skills and good habits through which children will be able to extend the reach of their learning in later years. We know that children will be less likely to live a productive adult life if they cannot read, write, and compute. Especially in the early grades, the best elementary school curricula are "unified" — one subject reinforces the next. Disciplinary borders vanish. Small children do not make fine distinctions between fairy tales and stories from history, between geography and science, and a skilled teacher can make each subject come alive by calling upon other knowledge the children are acquiring.

Our approach to the content of elementary curricula should reflect our conviction that the school is an agency of the entire adult community, that its goals should reflect the beliefs and priorities of the community at large. Elementary schools, says Study Group member Jean Marzollo, should be the place where children get exposed to "the good stuff." If they are besieged by tawdry fare in other places, they should find in school a curriculum that not only teaches them basic skills, but also exposes them to interesting ideas, beautiful images, and the adventures of men and women who lived in years gone by. Schools should compete for the attention of the mind and heart by offering the best we have. In the marketplace of ideas, schools should present a quality product. Cheaper goods are available elsewhere.

The branches to be studied, and the extent to which they are studied, will be determined mainly by the demands of one's own civilization. These will prescribe what is most useful to make the individual acquainted with physical nature and with human nature, so as to fit him as an individual to perform his duties in the several institutions — family, civil society, the state, and the church.   *—1895*

First and foremost, elementary schools must provide the **fundamental skills** with which to manage a lifetime of learning — abilities learned in what Study Group member Lauren Resnick calls the "enabling disciplines."

Reading

The elementary school must assume as its sublime and most solemn responsibility the task of teaching every child in it to read. Any school that does not accomplish this has failed. There is no excuse for the illiteracy and semi-literacy we are finding in our high schools and colleges, though there is a powerful **explanation** for this lamentable situation. The explanation, simply stated, is that some elementary schools — and responsible adults in other settings — have **failed** in their most basic responsibility: to send children forth into junior high, high school, and the adult world, reading fluently.

It is not as if we do not know how to achieve universal literacy among our young people. (Adult illiteracy is a subject for another discussion, but let me stipulate that   21 an ounce of prevention—applied in the elementary schools—is worth a pound of cure.) According to *Becoming A Nation of Readers*, the report of the Commission on Reading: "...[T]he last decade has witnessed unprecedented advances in knowledge about the basic processes involved in reading, teaching and learning. The knowledge is now available to make worthwhile improvements in reading throughout the United States."[6]

With all we know, we must not accept failure.

Yet too many of our children cannot read satisfactorily, even after 6 or 7 years of schooling. Consider a single sobering fact from *The Reading Report Card*, a report of the National Assessment of Educational Progress (NAEP). In 1984, among 13-year-olds, only three out of five were reading at the skill level appropriate for their age, defined by NAEP as the "ability to search for specific information, interrelate ideas, and make generalizations."[7] Virtually all of them possessed rudimentary reading skills. But forty 13-year-olds out of a hundred, 2 out of 5, lacked the "intermediate" reading skills that would enable them satisfactorily to handle the books and lessons that a seventh- or eighth-grade teacher should be able to assign. Worse, **most** minority youngsters (65 percent of blacks, 61 percent of Hispanics) were reading below the intermediate level in 1984.[8]

> *Reading should be both silent and oral.... Furthermore, prose and poetry, of an appropriate character, should be read to the classes throughout the grades in which pupils are too young to read such literature themselves.* —1895

When and where to begin? Children get a head start if parents and other adults read to them at home, and if they are exposed to stories and books from an early age. According to the Commission's report, a program combining both formal and informal instruction can begin as early as kindergarten—if it is "systematic but free from undue pressure."[9]

Most children are ready to read by first grade and, when formal instruction begins, the teaching method is of great significance. From the 1920s until the early 1970s, a method called "look-say" prevailed in American elementary schools; it relies on memorizing the meaning and appearances of entire words. But research of the past two decades has confirmed what experience and common sense tell us: that children learn to read more effectively when they first learn the relationship between letters and sounds. This is known as **phonics**.

Phonics helps most children, particularly those at high risk for learning to read. According to the Commission on Reading, "The right maxims for phonics are: Do it early. Keep it simple. Except in cases of diagnosed individual need, phonics instruction should have been completed by the second grade."[10] Yet, writes Study Group member Jeanne Chall, director of Harvard's Reading Laboratory and a member of the Commission on Reading: "It may be necessary to extend instruction in phonics for those who need it. The point of phonics is to help kids break the code. They arrive at school with substantial speaking and listening vocabularies; phonics helps

22

them make the connection between what they already know and the symbols they see on the page."

Some claim that a big source of reading problems is the deadening quality of what children are given to read. Children who go through the considerable work of learning to read can lose their appetite for it if all they get is drab monosyllabic vignettes in "readers." According to a Department of Education study, elementary schools tend to use basal readers up to the later grades—far beyond the point for which they were originally intended.[11]

There is nothing inherently wrong with reading collections; indeed, it makes great sense for early readers to provide sequential degrees of difficulty. But what is in these collections? Some publishers have produced versions of Aesop's *Fables*, the Brothers Grimm, and other classics which retain the dramatic qualities of language while coping with limited reading skills. Others have featured brief biographies, or poetry, and even the works of contemporary storytellers like Isaac Bashevis Singer. The editors and publishers of these imaginative and thoughtful children's works deserve much credit.

But, sadly, some other reading series are stultifying. As the Commission on Reading concluded: "Large publishing companies invest upwards of $15,000,000 to bring out new basal reading programs. Within budgets of this size, surely it is possible to hire gifted writers who can create stories far superior to the standard fare. The Commission believes that the American people ought to expect and should demand better reading primers for their children."[12] I believe that, too. We do not feed pablum to children who are ready for meat and vegetables, and we should not feed verbal pablum to children able to digest literature.

Children learn to read by reading—and schools should provide plenty of opportunities for them to do so. Yet one study shows that in the typical primary-school class, only 7 or 8 minutes per day are allotted to silent reading time.[13] Children spend about 70 percent of the time allocated for reading instruction engaged in "seatwork," mostly on skill sheets and workbooks that may require only a perfunctory level of reading.[14]

Properly integrated with other lessons, workbooks can be a useful adjunct to the learning process. But many of them do little to build reading or reasoning skills and, when handed out as busywork, they may even undermine children's respect for real thinking.

Reading is so much more than a skill to be polished through rote exercises. It is a passport to new worlds. Child psychologist Bruno Bettleheim urges that children read classic fairy tales, a rich source of symbols and episodes by which children may draw meaning for their own lives. Bettleheim says: "More can be learned from them about the inner problems of human beings, and of the right solutions to their predicaments in any society, than from any other type of story within a child's comprehension."

> *Literary works of art...portray situations of the soul, or scenes of life, or elaborated reflections, of which the child can obtain some grasp through his capacity to feel and think although in scope and compass they far surpass his range. They are adapted therefore to lead him out of and beyond himself, as spiritual guides.* —1895

Books should be a part of every child's life. They should occupy a central place in home and classroom alike. Children should have at their fingertips books like *Where the Wild Things Are, Charlotte's Web,* and *Winnie the Pooh.* This is the only way they will really grasp the idea that reading is a joy rather than a burden. Yet in a recent study of fifth-graders' reading habits, 90 percent of the children were found to read books only 4 minutes a day or less.[15] The same children may watch television an average of 3 ½ hours a day.

It is vitally important that children acquire solid reading skills early on, not only so they can begin to savor literature, but also so they can achieve success in school. Research shows that children who experience school failure often begin to have serious problems around fourth grade, when they must start applying their reading skills in earnest to other academic subjects.

One thing that may turn children away from reading is the dubious literary quality of their other textbooks. (As Study Group member Jo Gusman observes: "No one ever gave a child a textbook for Christmas.") In creating texts for history and science and math, publishers commonly employ "readability formulas" which attempt to gear vocabulary and sentence structure to grade levels. These formulas have some utility. As Professor Chall points out: "Studies of adult and child reading have found that what they read for their own pleasure depends on the readability of the material—not too easy or too hard." Yet chopping texts into small words and short sentences can rob them of beauty and sense. Textbook analyst Harriet Tyson-Bernstein notes that the word "because" does not show up in most American textbooks before the eighth grade. And, she adds, "you can imagine what that does to the text."[16] Writing that flows may be easier for children to comprehend. Certainly it will be more interesting.

One point cannot be repeated too emphatically: Children must have access to books. Every elementary school should have a library. Every **classroom** should have its own mini-library or reading corner. And parents and schools should make sure children know how to use the public library: A guided tour of it should be part of kindergarten.

Writing

The National Assessment of Educational Progress (NAEP) recently reported some awful, if not altogether surprising, news about our children's ability to write: Most of them can't—not nearly well enough.

According to NAEP, 91 percent of 13-year-olds were unable to write an adequate persuasive letter; 84 percent of 13-year-olds (and virtually all 9-year-olds) were unable to write an adequate imaginative essay; 81 percent of 13-year-olds (and

97 percent of 9-year-olds) couldn't produce a simple factual description requiring no opinion, creative thinking, or argumentation.[17]

How can this be? One answer is that we have come to confuse writing with filling in little blanks. Though many elementary schools have adopted inventive programs to encourage writing throughout the curriculum, the "writing" done in other elementary schools is really penmanship.

While it is essential that young children learn to form their letters and make individual words, those rudimentary skills should give way to the organization and expression of ideas just as soon as the child is ready. Writing should be part of the teaching strategy in every subject, not just "language arts." By the time they reach the upper elementary grades, children should be asked to compose essays about science projects and write biographical sketches of historical figures. They should even be asked to write about how they solve mathematical problems, and to put the solutions to word problems into full sentences. By the end of eighth grade, children should be writing more extended compositions, including some that call upon them to draw information from several sources. They should write and write and write some more, until it becomes second nature to put pencil—or printer—to paper and produce something coherent and expressive.

> *Learning to read and write should be the leading study of the pupil in his first four years of school. Reading and writing are not so much ends in themselves as means for the acquirement of all other human learning. This consideration alone would be sufficient to justify their actual place in the work of the elementary school.*   —1895

Researchers Carl Bereiter and Marlene Scarmadalia make a useful distinction between writing as "knowledge-telling" and writing as "knowledge-transforming."[18] It is essential that children understand, even in elementary school, that writing is more than the disgorging of information; it is the reorganization and transmission of knowledge through revision, editing, and rewriting.

If children need to write more, and need to get rapid and thorough feedback on what they produce, suitable provision must be made. The elementary teacher, with 25 students or so, is somewhat less pressed for time than the high school English teacher who may end up with 125 papers to review every time an assignment is given; but the elementary teacher may need a hand, too. Fortunately, not all responses have to come from the regular classroom teacher. Some school systems hire aides for this purpose. Others enlist volunteers. What a splendid opportunity for the community of adults to lend a hand to the teacher, and what better cause than fostering the emergence of a generation of adults who can communicate effectively in writing!

Besides ensuring ample feedback, school administrators can reinforce the notion that writing is important and rewarding by seeing that young authors get suitable recognition. Essays should hang on classroom and corridor walls. Awards may be bestowed on unusually good papers. Student compositions can be read aloud. These are some of the simple, practical steps that will help build the skills and experience children need.

Mathematics

Everyone agrees that math is a "basic." Yet American students are doing poorly in this subject. A recent study by the International Association for the Evaluation of Education Achievement (IEA) showed American eighth-graders scoring 13th among 17 countries studied.[19] Another study by Harold Stevenson and his associates found the **highest**-scoring American fifth-grade classrooms failing to match even the **lowest**-scoring Japanese classrooms.[20]

Why? Insufficient time in class doesn't seem to be the main problem; the Association for Supervision and Curriculum Development (ASCD) says fourth-graders get an average of 52 minutes of math per day.[21] But according to the National Council of Teachers of Mathematics, the curriculum at grade eight is still dominated by arithmetic computation whereas, by grade seven, Japanese and European children are already moving into algebra, geometry, and mathematical problem-solving.[22] Members of the Mathematics Sciences Education Board (sponsored by the National Academy of Sciences) blame a lack of emphasis on mastery: Children are presented the same material several times during their elementary years, instead of getting it conclusively and then moving on.[23]

> *The seventh and eighth years should be given to the algebraic method of dealing with those problems that involve difficulties in the transformation of quantitative indirect functions into numerical or direct quantitative data.* —1895

In the early grades, children learn mathematics best when they can manipulate physical objects in their lessons. Although very young children tend to think in concrete terms, a University of Chicago project shows that teachers can also introduce abstract math concepts into the early grades by using everyday phenomena. (For example, decimals can be introduced to first-graders by talking about units of money, and negative numbers can be introduced to kindergarten students by observation of an outdoor thermometer.) [24]

What is most lacking in elementary mathematics is a sense of relationship between the formal skills children learn and their application to real problems. Even as late as eighth grade, according to IEA, the teaching of math is "predominantly formal with an emphasis on rules, formulas, and computational skills as opposed to being informal, intuitive, and exploratory."[25]

How often, as adults, are we presented with formal computational assignments? We use math to **solve problems**, and each problem may involve a different set of specific functions. When we order from a menu, we estimate the costs of various combinations. If we choose a long-distance phone company, we perform dozens of discrete calculations. When we struggle over income taxes, we must choose and execute the right kinds of computation, perhaps hundreds of times in succession.

Children in the elementary years need not only the basic computing skills, but need also to learn how to select the right strategies to solve complicated problems. Our schools face a major challenge in imparting these crucial math skills and problem-solving strategies.

Science

The National Science Foundation recently disclosed a startling level of "scientific illiteracy" among American adults.[26] By far the highest rates of scientific misunderstanding occur among those who did not finish high school—perhaps indicating that their elementary education failed to equip them with basic concepts of scientific thinking.

> *Even arithmetic is not an inexorable threat to happiness when responsible experiences provide numerous contacts with things that need to be arranged, grouped, counted, compared, distributed, assembled, shared, bought, weighed, and measured.* —1948

We need a revolution in elementary-school science. There is probably no other subject whose teaching is so at odds with its true nature. We have come to think of science as a grab-bag of esoteric facts and stunts—the periodic table, the innards of frogs, the way to make little hot plates out of tin cans and wires. Worse, we have also given students the impression that science is a dry and arcane matter gleaned solely from the pages of a textbook. In three major studies, the National Science Foundation found that most science education follows the traditional practice: "At all grade levels the predominant method of teaching was recitation (discussion) with the teacher in control, supplementing the lesson with new information (lecturing). The key to the information and basis for reading assignments was the textbook."[27] If science is presented like this, is it any wonder that children's natural curiosity about their physical world turns into boredom by the time they leave grade school—and into dangerous ignorance later on?

Science is a way of thinking, a way of understanding the world. The term "scientific method" has fallen into disfavor among educators, perhaps because it conjures up images of a white-coated man hunched over a Petri dish. It ought to be restored. The scientific method is the method of thought, of reasoning, which applies not only to explorations of the physical universe but to all the realms of intellectual inquiry that require hypothesis, inference, and other tools of brainwork. As Bertrand Russell explained: "A fact, in science, is not a mere fact, but an instance."

Seen only as a laundry list of theorems in a workbook, science can be a bore. But as a "hands-on" adventure guided by a knowledgeable teacher, it can sweep children up in the excitement of discovery. Taught by the regular classroom teacher, it can illustrate the point that science is for everyone—not just scientists.

*Anne Beers School, in the District of Columbia, is the site of a demonstration project designed by the National Science Teachers Association and the D.C. Public Schools. An entire wing of the school has been designated its science center, and at any time of the school day children there are looking through microscopes, digging into dirt samples, discussing the difference between jungles and forests, telling each other how to work a telescope—**learning** science by **doing** science. It is a wonderful place, teaching wonderful things.*

Can this type of program be duplicated around the country? Anne Beers School has persuaded businesses and the community to support its program. There is no reason why local businesses elsewhere can't pitch in to provide lab equipment—indeed, why communities cannot form co-ops to supply materials for "hands-on" projects. Here is a place where business, industry, science centers, and universities can all help.

Today, science gets shortchanged in the typical elementary school, beginning with the simple matter of time. According to the ASCD, fourth-graders have only 28 minutes per day allocated to science,[28] and that is **allocated** time. In reality, they may receive a lot less instruction: The National Science Teachers Association points out that teachers often use discretionary time for subjects with which they are more comfortable—like reading and language arts.

> *Natural science claims a place in the elementary school, not so much as a disciplinary study, side by side with grammar, arithmetic and history, as a training in the habits of observation and in the use of the technique by which such sciences are expounded.*   —1895

The problem of assessment also constrains the spread of "hands-on" science. It is relatively easy to test children's knowledge when they have been asked to memorize lists of data from a text. It is much harder to design tests that measure learning derived from direct experience; some school systems provide checklists of students' ability to perform experimental tasks. The challenge before science educators is to develop better means of measuring both factual knowledge and the kinds of understanding students acquire through activities. When that task is accomplished, a major roadblock to science achievement will have been removed.

Social Studies

How shall we introduce children to their world? What should they know of its past and its present?

By the end of eighth grade, we should certainly expect that our children will know the basic saga of American history and the stories of its great men and women; the sources of our form of government in the Greek, Judeo-Christian, Roman, and Enlightenment traditions; the contours and locations of the physical world, and the major features of international landscapes; essential facts of the world's major nations; and their rights and obligations as American citizens.

I do not presume, desirable though it would be, that youngsters completing grade eight will all possess sophisticated causal explanations of all these matters. But they should have absorbed the basic data, the main sequences and relationships that link the key facts, and some appreciation of the significance of it all.

Many elementary schools are failing to deliver these lessons, and major reform is needed. Many of today's children pick up bits of these lessons from an odd, amorphous grab-bag called "social studies," derived from such disciplines as anthropology, sociology, law, psychology, history, science, economics and geography. They are typically presented in the early grades through a sequence called "expanding environments," a matrix according to which most states and most major textbook publishers now arrange the presentation of social studies.

Expanding environments places the child at the center of the universe. Study of the world begins in kindergarten with "me;" in the first grade it expands to the study of the child's own family; in the second grade to the child's neighborhood; and in the third grade to the local community. Study Group member Diane Ravitch observes that this sequence was originally introduced during the Great Depression to make children more aware of the social and economic realities of the world in which they lived. Over the years, Ravitch adds, social studies in the early grades has come to focus almost exclusively on social science, leaving children little or no time for learning about the past or the world beyond their immediate environment.

In fact, this narrow conception of children's interests has scant foundation in research studies of how children actually learn. Children can learn amazing things if presented in language they fathom and in ways that engage their lively minds and imagination. What they need most is what every generation of young people needs: ways to find meaning in the world and insight into what other people have made of their lives. Over the years, gifted teachers have found that children love myths, fables, legends, tall tales, and biographies. Great stories help childen understand the world, past and present, and reach beyond the confines of their own immediate experience.

Students themselves seem bored with the way social studies is now taught. A 1980 survey in *Science Education Databook* reported that only 3 percent of 9-year-olds named social studies as their favorite subject, compared to 48 percent selecting mathematics and 24 percent language arts.[29]

I propose that "social studies" as presently constituted be transformed. It should teach the knowledge and skills needed for life in a democratic society through the interrelated disciplines of history, geography and civics.

Kindergarten Through Third Grade: Social Studies, Not Social Science

Since very young children do not readily grasp abstractions like "the past," the social studies curriculum in the primary grades should begin developing their   29 awareness of the world through play, games, map-making, discussion and dramatization of literature, and other kinds of active learning. The curriculum should build on children's interests and experiences—but without constricting the inquiry to their neighborhood or community (whose barriers they have already transcended through television and travel). Instead of learning about "neighborhood helpers" and the other relentlessly mundane characters in current curricula, children should be introduced to adventure stories about families that crossed the continents and oceans—including boat people of the East and West Coasts; fantastic tales that stretch the imagination and sense of wonder; legends about daring pioneers of past and present. The present social studies curriculum is too full of ersatz social science and too concerned about "social living." What our children need are lessons that explore unfamiliar possibilities, that play on their imaginative capacities while teaching core democratic values like respect for persons, property, and truth.

Producing a new social studies sequence for the early grades is no small order, but it can be done in a way that combines excitement with solid learning. Instead of concentrating only on children's immediate environs and experience, the social studies teacher should aim to construct a rich program that will build civic, historical, and geographic literacy.

Civic literacy starts with the child as a citizen of the school, then develops an understanding of the rights and responsibilities of all citizens. It also teaches children the purpose and function of rules, and imparts a sense of our national identity—that we are a nation of immigrants and live in a unique multicultural society.

Historical literacy grows from the study and discussion of myths, legends, fairy tales, Bible stories, and the biographies of outstanding men and women. It develops historical empathy through dramatization and other activities giving children an idea of "what it was like to be...."

Geographic literacy can be developed by teaching an understanding of place, location, direction, distance, relative size and shape, earth-sun relationships, and how to identify features in the environment.

An ordered sequence stressing these basic concepts in an atmosphere of creative play and imaginative adventure will prepare children for the more academically rigorous work they will begin in grade four.

Grades Four Through Eight: History, Geography, and Civics

By the time they are 9 and 10, children are ready for more formal study of history, geography, and civics. Whether the content of these courses is presented chronologically (e.g., the ancient world, the medieval world, the modern world) or in the form of area studies (Asian civilization, Western Europe, etc.), the important point is that social studies in the upper elementary grades should stress the continuity and correlations among these three disciplines. Teachers can do this by asking key questions: "What did the state expect of a citizen in those times, and how do we differ today?" "What rights did a citizen have?" "How did people from that area travel to our country?"

Let us consider in a bit more detail the three pillars of elementary social studies curricula.

History

Though education critics are frequently faulted for imagining a "golden age" that never really existed, in the field of history it turns out that there truly was such a time. In the first quarter of the twentieth century, most American schools offered a history course in every grade. The history curriculum in the elementary years was largely fashioned upon the recommendations of a 1909 report by the Committee of Eight of the American Historical Association.

According to Diane Ravitch: "the Committee's proposals organized what was already commonplace in most American schools into a regular pattern. In the first three grades, the Committee recommended the teaching of Indian life and legends, stories about Columbus, George Washington and other heroes, heroes of other lands, the celebration of national, state, and local holidays, and the stories evoked by the holidays. Thanksgiving became a time to learn about the Pilgrims; Memorial Day was a time to learn about the Civil War."

This may sound familiar. Many of today's schools make paper turkeys at Thanksgiving and do reports on Columbus. But an elementary history curriculum in the late 20th century should consist of more than commemoration; it should develop rigorous knowledge based in a celebration of our own heritage. All year long, children should experience legends such as Paul Bunyan and Johnny Appleseed, should hear true stories of Revolutionary era heroes like Benjamin Banneker and Nathan Hale, should learn how women like Harriet Beecher Stowe and Emily Dickinson shaped the sensibilities of our young republic. Having acquired a clear sense of our own national traditions, students will possess the knowledge with which to compare our progress as a nation with that of other societies.

> *That the history of one's own nation is to be taught in the elementary school seems fixed by common consent.* —1895

If we are to restore the place of history in elementary curricula, specific standards will need to be set. But the experts have already helped us to understand what these should be. The Organization of American Historians says that by the end of eighth grade, children should:

- Know the basic chronology of the main events of U.S. history, and be able to place in order and roughly date the major periods of world history; 31

- Be able to explain the significance of the most important events in U.S. and world history — including social and economic developments that evolve over time, such as industrialization, slavery, urbanization, women's suffrage, and civil rights;

- Recognize and place in context some of the important men and women in U.S. history; and

- Have read and understood the essential significance of at least parts of such documents as the Declaration of Independence, the Constitution, Lincoln's Second Inaugural Address, and Martin Luther King's 'I Have A Dream' speech.[30]

As the historians point out, the words "significance," "context," and "understanding" are important; children should know the facts, yes, but should also know what ties them together.

In his 1986 Jefferson Lecture, sponsored by the National Endowment for the Humanities, philosopher Leszek Kolakowski warned of the "withering away" of historical consciousness. We are ushering in an epoch, he said, "when children, from the earliest age, will sit at their computers and, as a result, their minds will be entirely shaped by the acts of calculation, with historical self-understanding sinking into irrelevance or oblivion."

We can challenge this bleak scenario by insisting that history regain its rightful place in the elementary school curriculum. Lest we become complacent about this task, we should recall what C.S. Lewis wrote in *The Screwtape Letters*, as the devil Screwtape urges his nephew and protege Wormwood to cultivate in men a disdain for the past: "Since we cannot deceive the whole human race all the time," he says, "it is important to cut every generation off from all the others; for where learning makes a free commerce between the ages, there is always a danger that the characteristic errors of one may be corrected by the characteristic truths of another." It is to the maintenance of that "free commerce between the ages" that the teaching of history is crucial.

> *The educational value of geography, as it is and has been in elementary schools, is obviously very great. It makes possible something like accuracy in the picturing of distant places and events, and removes a large tract of mere superstition from the mind.* —1895

Geography

Once an important part of the elementary curriculum, geography has suffered great neglect. A 1983 study of 12-year-olds in eight industrialized countries found American students especially lacking in basic geographic knowledge. (In one test group, 20 percent of the students could not even locate the United States on a world map.)[31] A 1984 survey of North Carolina college students' geographic knowledge found 95 percent "flunking" — that is, scoring less than 70 percent. Only 27 percent of the students knew that the Amazon River was in Brazil, and a mere 20 percent associated the Ganges with India. Of those responding, 71 percent "never had reference to geography in their elementary schooling."[32]

Just as in the study of history, we recognize that children need to develop certain cognitive skills before they can handle abstract geographic concepts like "north" and "south." But they can begin at an early age to learn illustrations of the five basic themes of geography education: location, place, relationships within places, movement, and regions.

The National Geographic Society has recently made a commendable commitment to the restoration of geography instruction in elementary education. Through books, films, and slides, the Society is fostering the idea that geography can give children a sense of people and place; can promote the habit of detailed observation; can heighten reasoning and deductive thinking; and can familiarize children with the environments in which they and other people live. The Society also provides a good example of how simple ideas can be helpful: It has produced a beach ball in the shape of a globe. While throwing or kicking it around, children learn where the oceans and continents are!

Civics

American civics, like American history, should be presented without sugarcoating but also without apology. This is not chauvinism. The proper first focus of study by American boys and girls, regardless of ancestry or ethnicity, is on the essential facts, the central institutions, and the fundamental principles of the United States and the western civilization whose traditions and culture are our shared inheritance. Harry Truman said it well: "You see the future of this great country depends entirely on the coming generations and their understanding of what they have and what was done to create it, and what they must do to keep it."[33]

Contemporary educators would do well to look at a 1941 publication of the National Education Association entitled *The American Citizens Handbook*. Not only does it provide the texts of such significant documents as the Magna Carta, the Mayflower Compact, and Lincoln's Second Inaugural Address; it also states plainly and forthrightly that American children ought to know and understand their civic heritage. About our Constitution, for example, it says: "Every American should know its content. It is the greatest single document in the entire struggle of mankind for orderly self-government."

> *A good elementary school must have skilled teachers deeply versed in the democratic ideal.*
>
> — *1948*

Our elementary schools should nurture children's appreciation for these cornerstones of their democracy. Sound educational practice would ensure that children become well-grounded in the lore of their own land before embarking upon comparative studies of other histories, cultures, societies, and   33 governments. Else they will have no basis from which to understand similarities and differences.

One way of introducing these civic concepts is to view the school as a community unto itself. Many elementary schools now have codes of conduct and procedures through which students can adjudicate infractions; "banks" that make loans for school projects; elections for class officers and student council. These are activities that can make vivid the rights and responsibilities of democratic citizenship.

It is especially important that history and civics be taught to children who are new to America. The threads of our civic tradition—our laws, our culture, our institutions—have bound together the American quilt for generations now; our liberties continue to beckon those who suffer. As our schools welcome the children of families who have fled Castro and Duvalier and Pol Pot, we must not abandon the teaching of our American traditions in the name of "globalism" or "multiculturalism." Instead, we must be ready to hand these newcomers the instruction manual for our pluralist democracy. As historian Stephan Thernstrom has eloquently written: "It is time ... for the schools to pay more heed to the *Unum* in the motto on the seal of the United States—*E Pluribus Unum*. When it was adopted in 1782, the phrase referred to the forging of a single nation out of the original 13 colonies, but it has since come to refer as well to the binding together of so many diverse peoples into one. For all of our differences we have long had a common national history and a common national identity, a feeling for what Abraham Lincoln called the mystic cords of memory that bind successive generations of Americans together."[34]

Cultural Literacy

"Cultural literacy" may sound like a narrow concern of budding humanities scholars, but it is an essential frame for the skills and knowledge developed in the social studies curriculum, as well as in other subjects. E.D. Hirsch and other scholars have found that children do less well in school if they do not possess a body of shared knowledge about references and symbols. A great problem for those who design tests, for example, is that minority and non-English proficient students may lack certain kinds of knowledge taken for granted among the majority population. Yet the problem is not limited to minorities. Children of any economic or linguistic group who get most of their cultural information from television may know a great deal about rock stars and nothing about Lewis and Clark; may be able to name seven of the top hitters in the National League, but not seven of the last ten presidents; may know more about the processing of cocaine than about the chemical composition of table salt. A principal function of elementary school must be to introduce children to the "common knowledge" of our shared culture.

> *The schools in a democracy must continue to obtain their direction from the people they serve. This direction finds its source not only in laws but in the traditions and culture of the people themselves.* —1953

34

The Arts

The arts are an essential element of education, just like reading, writing, and arithmetic.

J. Carter Brown, Director of the National Gallery of Art, explains their central importance: "The texts of man's achievements are not written exclusively in words. They are written, as well, in architecture, paintings, sculpture, drawing, photography, and in urban, graphic, landscape, and industrial design."[35]

Music, dance, painting, and theater are keys that unlock profound human understanding and accomplishment. Children should be handed these keys at an early age. Yet, according to the Council of Chief State School Officers, boards of education in only 13 states specified the arts within formal statements of educational goals as of September 1985.[36] A study by George Hardiman and Andra Johnson in *Art Education* found that elementary schools commit only 4 percent of their school week to art instruction, with only a quarter of that provided by trained art teachers.[37]

An elementary school that treats the arts as the province of a few gifted children, or views them only as recreation and entertainment, is a school that needs an infusion of soul. Children's imaginations yearn for the chance to transcend the ordinary, to hear and see what they have not heard and seen before. The Task Force for the Fine Arts in Baltimore's school system says, "Every student should have the opportunity to explore the arts as *systems of meaning*—as a living history of people and as a record and revelation of the human spirit."[38]

Yet today, children's access to the arts often takes the form of unstructured "fun time." Finger-painting and playing on flutophones may be terrific ways of getting young children to try art—but curricula which feature such activities to the exclusion of Mozart and Michelangelo underestimate students' capacities.

Some elementary educators take seriously their responsibility to provide the "good stuff" kids might not get elsewhere. Real arts instruction does not have to be heavy or solemn; just look at the excitement stirred up by Jacques d'Amboise in his dance programs for New York City's schools! And hear what happens at the Kennedy Center when the National Symphony performs *Peter and the Wolf*. Children respond rapturously when exposed to quality in the arts.

> *The reading and study of fine selections in prose and verse furnish the chief aesthetic training of the elementary school. But this should be re-enforced by some study of photographic or other reproductions of the world's great masterpieces of architecture, sculpture, and painting.*
>
> *—1895*

The Getty Foundation has established a program to promote the arts in America's elementary schools. They call it "Beyond Creating"— stressing that proper arts education should include not only activities but also, from an early age, instruction in historical and critical understanding. A sequential program, gradually expanding the base of knowledge and including performance, can add immeasurably to a child's capacity for appreciation. Teachers can help establish a proper balance between experience and theory.

We would all benefit by seeing arts education in a larger context. For one thing, the arts can give coherence, depth, and resonance to other academic subjects. Professor Elliot Eisner of Stanford University notes that intellectual skills cultivated by art education "not only represent the mind operating in its finest hour but are precisely the skills that characterize our most complex adult life tasks."[39]

Foreign Languages

Children learn languages most effectively when instruction begins early and continues throughout schooling. We know this is true of English; it is also true of other languages. Yet the elementary school that offers a full foreign language program remains the exception rather than the rule. Should we then seek to broaden foreign language teaching?

Indiana Governor Robert Orr, a Study Group member, thinks so. In view of the realities of the world economy, he regards foreign language as one of the "new basics." Certainly, foreign language instruction is a good way to introduce children to other cultures—and to stimulate their understanding of geography and history.

The question often put to advocates of foreign language instruction is: What language should be taught at the elementary level? It is not surprising that young students in Europe and the USSR learn English; ours is now the primary language of international commerce and diplomacy. But should American students learn Russian, or Spanish, or Urdu?

Let's not become preoccupied with that question. What is important is for students, early on, to "break the language barrier"—to grasp the fact that any language, including English, is a way of communicating, of conveying meaning. Young students can use any second language to break out of the monolingual habit. In fact, a number of school districts have begun offering Latin at the elementary level, in some cases using it to help disadvantaged students get a better grip on English. What matters is not so much that students master any specific tongue; what they should learn at the elementary level is that they can learn—that foreign language need not be alien territory.

Health and Physical Education

Do children get enough exercise by careening around a playground at lunchtime? Some do. Some kids burn energy like a '58 Buick. Some are always moving.
But look closely at a grade school playground, and you will probably see a few youngsters off to the side, barely moving a muscle. It is for these boys and girls, as well as for the well-being of their more active friends, that an orderly program

of health and physical education is a must. The President's Council on Physical Fitness and Sports says that American children are in remarkably bad shape: 40 percent of boys age 6 to 12 cannot do more than one pull-up; one in four cannot do any. Seventy percent of girls age 6 to 12 cannot do more than one pull-up; 55 percent cannot do any. In a 50-yard dash, today's 10-year-old girls are "significantly" slower than those tested 10 years ago.[40] According to Council chairman George Allen: "Most of today's adults had a taste of fitness from their phys-ed classes in school before phys-ed was dropped.... But today's kids don't get that taste of fitness now when they're young."[41]

Such programs belong in elementary schools not only because they promote health and well-being, but because they contribute tangibly to academic achievement. Researchers in France, Australia, Israel, and the United States have all found that youngsters who partake in structured programs of vigorous exercise possess greater mental acuity and stronger interest in learning than those who do not.[42]

Best of all, most children like sports and look forward to a well-planned gym period or physical education class. Capitalizing on this youthful enthusiasm, San Diego has organized some of its elementary magnet schools with a dual focus on science/mathematics and physical education. The track meets and fitness programs draw some youngsters who then succumb to the science lab, too!

Health and nutrition education should also be a part of the elementary curriculum. Children should learn how their bodies function, what kinds of food to eat, how to avoid illness, and what the disastrous effects of drug use will be. Maintaining children's good health is a shared responsibility of parents, schools, and the community at large. But elementary schools have a special mandate: to provide children with the knowledge, habits, and attitudes that will equip them for a fit and healthy life.

> *Systematic physical training has for its object rather the will-training than recreation, and this must not be forgotten. To go from a hard lesson to a series of calisthenic exercises is to go from one kind of will-training to another.* —1895

The School Health Curriculum Project (SHCP), a cooperative venture of five federal agencies, recently surveyed nearly 1,100 fourth- to seventh-grade classrooms using four popular health programs. The study found that "schools have much to contribute to the classic ideal of a sound mind in a sound body. Well-designed programs can affect subsequent student knowledge, attitudes, and—most important— behavior...." And SHCP found that the gains are greatest when schools devote ample time to health education.[43]

Computers

Computers can be a major resource in helping a school accomplish its central educational missions. But "computer literacy" is a useful skill, not an end in itself.   37

Study Group member Cecil Good, Executive Director of Instructional Technology for the Detroit public schools, says computers can "jazz up" the teaching of writing. Word-processing programs allow children to experiment with language, try different sentence structures, and revise without huge effort. Other programs can teach musical concepts; make mathematics a visible, concrete experience; and add new scope to the sciences. As the Carnegie Corporation reports: "There are school labs where fourth graders learn some fundamental principles of engineering by designing, programming and building computer-controlled devices that make use of light sensors to guide motor-driven vehicles."[44]

Computers can also extend the reach of classroom teachers by relieving them of clerical chores and by promoting individualized instruction. At Willis Junior High in Arizona, members of the Study Group saw a remarkable program for bilingual instruction, in which Spanish-speaking children were learning English via computer programs that responded to their individual capabilities. For a single teacher to deliver this kind of tutorial instruction to a large class would require masterful planning—and a pair of running shoes.

Computers can even help pay for themselves. Eighth-graders in Willis' advanced computer class handle some of the school's clerical work, noting inventories and performing other routine tasks. Not only is this an illustration of how computers work—it is a dandy method of introducing children to some real-world applications of their lessons.

For rural educators, computers can be a special blessing. Through computer networks, schools in isolated areas can get access to new research and information about innovative teaching techniques. Where teachers are in short supply, computer technology can provide a critical level of individual attention for children receiving special education and other services.

Libraries

Youngsters need ready access to books. The school library is evolving these days, and the currently fashionable title is "library media center." I'm a little wary of this term. While it is true that in this high-technology world, our children must discover early on how to get access to information, and should certainly learn how to conduct independent research, it is of critical importance that girls and boys acquire the habit of **reading**. School libraries should find children reading biographies and histories and novels and science fiction—not simply looking for a fugitive fact or random quotation. The librarian should be an integral part of the instructional staff. By leading children to good books, by sponsoring incentive programs and author visits, the librarian can play an essential role in enriching curricula.

Video, film, and recordings convey information, too. All serve as teaching tools and can be especially useful in opening the doors to literacy for students with learning problems or limited English skills. But my hope is that for most students, these essentially passive media would take second place to books and other reading material at the elementary level. In league with classroom teachers, the librarian can foster in children a taste for good literature and a love of serious study. Good librarians can be great teachers.

And children should **belong** to the public library. There is one within striking distance of practically everybody. Let's have a national campaign: By the end of the 1986-87 school year, every child should obtain a library card—and use it.

The Implicit Curriculum

Through science and history, through math and geography, students pursue the explicit goals of schooling. But schools also have another powerful "curriculum": the implicit lessons they deliver concerning the development of character and morality.

In the words of social philosopher Russell Kirk, "...A rough age requires some people possessed of an energetic virtue."[45] One place children will discover models of such virtue is in biographies and adventure stories. Through books that have stood the test of time, children imbibe enduring lessons of courage, conscience, and enterprise. For very young children, powerful first lessons can even be found in fairy tales. As Study Group member Jeanne Chall wrote in *Learning to Read: The Great Debate*: "...I have never found [a child] who could not identify with Cinderella, The Gingerbread Boy, or The Three Little Pigs. These tales contain struggle and triumph, right and wrong, laughter and tears—themes that have disappeared from modern stories based on familiar experiences."[46]

> *The higher moral qualities of truth-telling and sincerity are taught in every class exercise that lays stress on accuracy of statement."*
>
> *—1895*

Since a primary goal of American elementary education is the development of democratic citizenship, an essential part of the implicit curriculum is each school's interpretation of its responsibility to provide civic education—not only in textbooks and lectures, but through saluting the flag, singing the national anthem, and other rituals of our national life. Parents might look for more subtle displays of burgeoning democracy as well: Does the school draw on the diversity of its students in celebrating our pluralist heritage? Does it provide trips to the courts, the mayor's office, the town hall? Does it pause to honor the men and women who fought in foreign wars, and explain what they were fighting for? These are all ways in which schools can build citizenship on a daily basis.

Finally, the implicit curriculum flows from the behavior of a school's own adult population. Study Group member Edgar Nease says, "Values are 'caught' more than taught." This is why we require that those who teach our children be of good character and understand that they are a potent influence on children's development. As Aristotle and William James both reminded us, character is acquired through habit. If children

39

see teachers and principals as models of democratic sensibilities, they will tend to build the right kind of habits.

It happened that on the day the shuttle Challenger exploded, members of the Study Group were visiting Avon Elementary in central Indiana. Later, Rita Kramer wrote of watching one teacher break the tragic news to her students: "She told them quietly and not hiding her own sadness, but she didn't go to pieces either. Taking their cue from her, the children followed their initial moments of shock and grief—even tears—with talk of the children whose parents had been killed and then thoughts of their own families and how they would feel if anything happened to them. An hour later they were calm, accepting. Not unfeeling, just reconciled to fate....Children react to life's vicissitudes, even its most horrible disasters, in ways suggested to them by the attitudes and comportment of the adults around them."

Will It All Fit?

With all these suggestions about reading and history, about art and computers, some educators are sure to object that no school can possibly accommodate all the improvements we need. I know that is not a simple issue. No school can transform itself overnight—but any school can begin to adopt strategies for getting where it needs to go. The total instructional program can be enlarged in a number of ways:

In order to find a place in the elementary school for the several branches recommended in this report, it will be necessary to use economically the time allotted for the school term, which is about 200 days, exclusive of vacations and holidays. Five days per week and five hours of actual school work or a little less per day, after excluding recesses for recreation, give about twenty-five hours per week. —1895

1) **Eke out more instructional time from the present schedule.** One reason overseas elementary schools outpace ours in international comparisons may be that other countries' children simply get in more learning time than ours do. Harold Stevenson's cross-cultural studies found American fifth-graders spending 64.5 percent of their school time on academic activities. By contrast, Chinese children spend 91.5 percent of their school hours on academics, and Japanese children, 87.4 percent. (Keep in mind that the Chinese and Japanese also put in more hours.)[47]

It is so well established by research and common sense as to sound foolish to repeat, but children tend to learn that which they spend time studying, and they tend to learn it in proportion to the amounts of time that they spend on it. Educators call this concept "academic learning time." Researchers have shown that this time can be enlarged through simple management techniques that any principal and teacher can employ. The principal can avoid cutting into class time for announcements and teacher meetings. (Both are important; both can be done outside regular class hours!) Professor David Berliner of the University of Arizona points out that if a teacher writes the next assignment on the board before the lunch break, students can get

40

started on it a few minutes sooner when they return to the classroom. Those few minutes add up.

2) **Use homework and other time-extenders.** Connecting homework more tightly to classroom instruction can free class time for new material. For example, teachers may wish to reserve class time for introducing new concepts, assigning drill and practice as homework once they're sure the children have grasped the new ideas.

3) **Employ creative curricular strategies.** To the extent that elementary curricula are "interconnected"—and that teachers have the time and guidance to coordinate their lesson plans with each other—schools can eliminate overlap and increase learning time. If state mandates allow, schools might consider covering fewer topics in greater depth, or adopting a case-method approach to some subjects.

4) **Free teachers to teach.** When teachers must oversee the playground, do clerical paperwork, monitor the cafeteria, and perform a host of other non-instructional functions, the time they can give to real instruction suffers. To free teachers for teaching, some schools employ aides and para-professionals. Others involve hundreds of parents in their activities—in some cases, even training parents to provide tutorial support. More professional instruction can be delivered if teachers are spared extraneous chores.

5) **Set school priorities and give parents choices among them.** Schools need not all assemble the curriculum into identical packages or give precisely the same weight to every element. So long as a minimum "core" is taught by every school in the district, why not encourage diversification and specialization, much as "magnet school" programs do today, and then permit parents to select the curricular emphases and instructional strategies they favor for their children?

6) **Consider lengthening the school year.** This solution is the most obvious, and is also the most likely to meet resistance. But for those schools wanting to create a truly complete curriculum for all their students, the calendar must be addressed. Consider that while most American children attend school for 180 days each year, Japanese children put in 240 days. Harvard Professor Thomas Rohlen says: "By high school graduation, Japanese children have been in school somewhere between three and four more years than their American counterparts."[48]

It was not always so. In the early 1800's, most American cities followed school schedules similar to the current Japanese model—259 days per year in Detroit; 235 days in New York; 251 days in Philadelphia. In the early twentieth century, schedules started shrinking.[49] Today, the long summer vacation is practically universal—although as the *Wall Street Journal* reports, about 425 American schools with an enrollment totalling 345,000 operate year-round.[50]

Westridge Elementary in Provo, Utah, is the first school in that state to adopt a year-round program. Here's how it works: Students are divided into four tracks. Each track takes a 15-day vacation after approximately 45 days of school—or four good-sized vacations per year. Traditional holidays are also observed. Forty per-   41 *cent of the teachers teach year-round—225 days—while the rest teach 180 days. Principal John Bone says this system gives teachers the opportunity to make a higher salary; it saved the school $57,000 during the 1984-5 school year; and it helps take care of the need for more space.*[51]

R. Mac Irving, President of the Alabama Association of School Boards, points to a potential 25 percent increase in the efficiency of schooling: "Year-round education programs can produce a better return for taxpayers on their investment in school buildings and equipment.... Twelve-month schools will attract brighter students as teachers.... The potential benefits are too great to allow the traditional arguments in favor of nine-month schools to prevail."[52]

Considering all the demands being made for stronger curricula, higher teacher pay, and added facilities to accommodate the "baby boomlet" of the next decade, this approach bears consideration. Most members of the Study Group urged me to endorse a longer school year, and I do— provided the time is well-used. There is considerable evidence that a four-quarter system leads to increased achievement through greater student retention of learned information. While it may require a rethinking of how we plan our vacations, that's a reasonable price to pay for the promise of more successful lives for our children.

Think of it another way. As Charles Ballinger, Executive Secretary of the National Council on Year-Round Education, asks: "If year-round education were the traditional school calendar, and had been for over 100 years, and if someone were to suggest a new school calendar whereby students would be exempted from formal instruction for up to three months at a time, would the U.S. public allow, or even consider, such a scheme?"[53]

Let us be clear, though, that what we need is not more time doing more of the same; we need more time spent more wisely. A longer school year does not void our responsibility to take out what deserves to be out and put in what deserves to be in. A longer school year should not be a means of satisfying everyone's views on everything, but evidence of a commitment to do what is essential for our students in the amount of time necessary to do it.

CHAPTER III:

ELEMENTARY SCHOOL PROFESSIONALS

The Principal

Among a number of good ideas in the recent Carnegie report on teaching, I believe there was one flawed notion: the idea that schools should be run by committees of "lead teachers," with principals more or less officiating. On the contrary: As Study Group member Sandy Wisley observes, "You won't find an excellent school without a strong principal."

If a school is to function as a "working community," if all the parts are to mesh in an engine of achievement, the principal must act as catalyst. More than any other figure, the principal is able to create conditions for excellence – or what Study Group member Michael Joyce calls "an ethos of shared expectations." Says Professor James Guthrie of the University of California-Berkeley: "[If] you could only change one component of a school in order to make it more effective, finding a dynamic principal is the most important thing you can do."[1]

There is a paradox at the heart of the principalship. Not only is the principal required to manage the business of the school; the successful principal also functions as an "instructional leader" – directing the actual teaching and learning process itself. This means working together with the teaching staff to implement academic goals; ensuring that order and discipline prevail; and making choices about materials and instructional strategies.

Every good principal develops his or her own version of instructional leadership. To Bruce Bernhardt, principal of Indiana's South Putnam Elementary School, it means supporting his veteran teaching staff – "finding 100 different ways to say 'good job.'" To Samuel Laitman, principal of P.S. 40 in Brooklyn's Bedford-Stuyvesant section, it means sending home "certificates of accomplishment" to parents who read with their children. To Jeremiah Kellett, of Woodland Elementary in Weston, Massachusetts, it means convening weekly staff conferences to discuss curricular and administrative issues.

A good elementary principal is ubiquitous, monitoring corridors, visiting classrooms, lunching with the children and staff. But in addition to duties within the school building, today's elementary school principal must occupy a position of visible leadership in the surrounding community. In the course of a week, a principal may be required to talk a local manufacturer into letting 50 fourth-graders tour his premises; testify before the school board as to why it should not eviscerate *Huckleberry Finn*; encourage the Chamber of Commerce to help buy new lab equipment; and give a talk to the Rotary about how the latest test scores turned out. And, as the National Association of Elementary School Principals notes, principals should "know how the media function, and make a point of becoming acquainted with education reporters who cover their school."[2]

Principals' relationships with parents are multidimensional. Since parent involvement is critical to school success, principals go to great lengths to enlist their support. But parents may also come to school with concerns about a teacher's performance or behavior, or with conflicts over values and beliefs. (Of course, the latter set of dilemmas can more readily be resolved if the school is one the parents chose for their child in the first place—and if they have the option of choosing a different one.) The principal's task in mediating between parent and teacher may be exceedingly hard. To succeed in it, he must be a diplomat, a negotiator, and a judge, with the patience of Job and the wisdom of Solomon.

Where do we find such virtuosos?

Nearly all of today's elementary school principals began their careers as teachers. In the absence of career ladders or other provisions for teachers to obtain professional advancement, the principalship has long been the teacher's main avenue to greater responsibility and higher pay.

We know that many effective principals are people who find ways to make end-runs around downtown (or upcounty) education bureaucracies, women and men who invent ingenious ways to get what their teachers and children need despite silly rules, rigid procedures, and empty coffers. But today's methods of educating and licensing principals seem better designed to produce survivors than entrepreneurs. Professors Bruce Cooper and William Boyd, who have studied the training and certification of school principals, say the process is "state-controlled, closed to non-teachers, mandatory for all those entering the profession, university-based, credit-driven, and certification-bound." While this process prevents "untrained charlatans from preying on the unsuspecting," it also, they say, "promotes mediocrity more than brilliance."[3] The elementary school of the future will demand a level of executive skill and imagination that may not be found often enough inside the corridors of education bureaucracies.

For this reason, **we should deregulate the principalship.** Of the 52,000 public elementary school principals in the United States today, more than half will be replaced by 1994.[4] I suggest that we look not only at exceptionally able educators, but also at men and women who have demonstrated leadership in other realms. A businessperson who has spent 20 years running a successful firm; a retired Army officer; the head of a government bureau; the publisher of a journal; the director of an art school—all these should be able to join the pool of prospective elementary

44

school principals, provided they possess the requisite personal qualities. Not having taught should not be an insuperable barrier.

Critics will argue that "outsiders" cannot possibly understand the dynamics of a classroom, or know enough about academic subjects to handle the instructional component of the principalship. As to the first contention, we can ensure enough familiarity with classroom procedure by means of intensive pre-service training and a carefully monitored apprenticeship. In this sense, I would require much more rigorous preparation for principals than is commonly the case today. As Chester Finn and Kent D. Peterson have written: "...Many a new principal is 'handed the keys' and given full responsibility for a building, even a cluster of buildings, without ever having engaged in the practice of school administration under the watchful eye and the supporting hand of a seasoned professional."[5] The Southern Regional Education Board proposes certification based on demonstrated skills and knowledge: "Beginning principals should be granted provisional certification until they successfully demonstrate on-the-job skills.... Managerial experience might be substituted for education courses."[6]

To be sure, there are areas of specialized knowledge in which all principals will need rigorous preparation: child development, curriculum organization, the application of research, and techniques for evaluating staff performance. But I believe this material can be learned in short intensive courses and well-structured apprenticeships, and through ample opportunities for mid-career renewal.

Attracting new blood into the principalship may not require much more money, either. A recent survey showed a range of median salaries for elementary school principals from a minimum of $33,256 to a maximum of $43,810—with a few districts paying much higher figures, up to a national maximum of $63,964.[7] Combine these respectable levels of compensation with a high degree of autonomy and a real opportunity to turn a school around, and we should be able to lure enough talented people into the field.

Saying that the training and education of elementary school principals needs to be improved is in no way a criticism of all those who now hold the position. The Department of Education's Elementary School Recognition Program has found hundreds of schools where principals' imaginative leadership has led to dramatic improvements. Members of the Study Group also met superlative principals—leaders who might succeed in any field. Elementary education is fortunate to have many like them in its ranks.

Teachers

People who believe that teaching an elementary school class is easy should try doing it. In the past year, I have taught classes in a number of elementary schools and I can attest that it is no simple task. The younger the child, the more difficult the challenge. I have unbounded admiration for the man or woman who spends 180 days a year teaching well in an elementary classroom. Life holds few greater rewards   45 than educating the next generation. Some misguided people make it sound as if it were demeaning to spend the day in a room full of elementary school children. It is surely demanding—to the point of exhaustion, in some cases—but most teachers find it deeply gratifying.

A recent study by the National Center for Education Information provided some keen insights into why people teach. According to NCEI Director Emily Feistritzer, "The vast majority of teachers are in that profession for all the reasons we hope they are. They say it themselves. When asked what is most important to them on a job, teachers say an opportunity to use their own minds and abilities and a chance to work with young people, followed by appreciation for a job well done."[8] This represents no recent burst of altruism, either. A study by Thomas Provenzo and associates showed only 14.2 percent of Dade County teachers listing salary as the primary reward of their profession in 1984—a figure nearly identical to the 14.3 percent who gave that answer in 1964.[9]

With a lot of experienced teachers retiring and with elementary school enrollments rising, close to a million new elementary-level teachers will be needed by 1993. But we are not, in fact, facing a crisis of numbers. As NCEI's Feistritzer points out, those million new teachers represent regular replacement at long-established rates of turnover and attrition. We might wish for greater stability in the ranks of teaching, and there will surely be "spot shortages" in particular specialties and communities. But that suggests the nature of the real challenge: not so much quantitative as qualitative. How do we organize ourselves to harvest a bumper crop of new teachers at a time when we are also demanding drastic improvement in the breadth and depth of their preparation?

Empowerment

At a meeting of the Study Group, Arizona State Senator Anne Lindeman observed that whenever state policymakers ask educators what reforms are needed, one answer always comes back: higher salaries. She's correct, of course; this answer is often heard. And in my judgment it is indeed part of the proper answer. In most places, entry-level salaries for teachers should be higher than they are today; outstanding veteran teachers should be paid more, too. The effect of these and other changes will be to boost the average salary. Indeed, that is just what has been happening in the United States, where average teacher salaries have increased by 23 percent in the past 3 years.[10] I applaud this trend, but let's understand that the principles of teacher compensation need reform, too. The essential point is to start paying teachers on the basis of quality rather than seniority, performance rather than tenure, merit rather than uniformity. It should be possible for a district's ablest teachers to earn salaries that rival those of lawyers and full professors. Such performance-linked gradations will have the effect of increasing the average, but through a completely different mechanism than an across-the-board raise.

46   We should encourage communities to look closely at their school budgets, as

well, to see whether classroom teachers are getting their proper share. One of the more perplexing and worrisome trends in education finance over the past decade has been the steady erosion of the teacher's portion of the public school dollar.

Let us also remind ourselves from time to time that money is not all or the most important thing that teachers value about their profession. Feistritzer's data are compelling, as are the results of many other polls. One such survey was recently conducted by *Instructor* magazine, which questioned its teacher readership expressly for the purpose of obtaining information for the Study Group and this report. When asked which one change would help raise the status of teaching, more than seven respondents in ten urged improved public understanding of their jobs, and other alterations related less to remuneration than to respect, autonomy, and professionalism.

Of the 8,000 mostly elementary teachers responding, not even 30 percent said that they make "most" of the important decisions related to texts and supplementary materials for their students. Forty-seven percent said they make "none" of the important decisions related to inservice training in their schools. Sixty-one percent had no opportunities to observe their colleagues teaching. A mere 24 percent said they were "meaningfully involved in choosing the subjects and grades that I teach." And only 16 percent "frequently" received useful guidance from the principal on instructional matters.[11]

Classroom materials provided to teachers may frustrate their attempts to judge what's best for their students—and thus may impede students' ability to learn. "Teacher manuals have docility embedded in the teachers' directions and questioning techniques," observes Study Group member Jo Gusman. "Answers are right, wrong, but mostly short, thus smothering the student's efforts to be an effective and intuitive thinker."

Is this any way to treat "professionals"? Although that is how teachers think of themselves—and it is a label richly merited by the dedication and effort of many in their ranks—the designation hardly fits the realities of teachers' lives today. Most teachers enjoy little control over the terms of their work, and have few opportunities to take initiatives to improve their own effectiveness. As Study Group member Dan Cheever points out: "Teaching has many of the same characteristics as other professions, including mastery of a body of knowledge. Yet it is denied important rights and responsibilities, such as setting its own standards for judging performance. We tell teachers what they should do, rather than listening to them define what needs to be done."

Instructor's Leanna Landsmann says this adds up to a desire for **empowerment** of teachers. I agree. Teachers should be assisted to become the professionals they want to be.

Preparation

The quest for teacher professionalism in the elementary schools runs into barriers. Because these schools have so long been located at the bottom of the education status hierarchy, "empowering" those who teach in them has not been high on the list of priorities of reformers and policymakers. Moreover, our conventional approach to the education of elementary school teachers has scarcely furnished them with the solid knowledge base on which true professionalism must ordinarily rest. Talk about getting things backwards! The elementary school teacher should be education's premier **generalist**, the one educator who is conversant with all the central disciplines and major subjects that form the core of the school enterprise. California school chief Bill Honig has termed elementary teachers the ambassadors whom the community of adults sends to the foreign shores of childhood, and has suggested that the best possible way to ascertain the adequacy of their education is to administer the Foreign Service Exam to them!

No high school teacher needs so broad a range of knowledge as does virtually every elementary teacher. Yet elementary teacher training programs remain the strongest bastion of the "methods course" and the "education major." What this means, practically speaking, is that the average elementary school teacher graduating from one of these programs has had little or no science, only a smattering of history, some electives in the humanities, and a number of courses featuring not academic material but rather, instruction on how to **present** academic material. (Instead of learning mathematics, in other words, they learn how to talk to fourth-graders about mathematics.) According to a 1981 survey by *Arithmetic Teacher* Magazine, only 34 percent of teacher colleges required more than one course in mathematics itself—while 90 percent required one or more "methods" courses.[12]

> *Whatever we wish to see in our children, we must be sure exists in the teachers of our children. We shall not develop a democratic citizenship in our elementary schools unless those schools are staffed with people who...possess a better than average degree of civic responsibility, people who could fill important positions in other occupations and at other educational levels.* —1948

The Southern Regional Education Board examined what it called "The Anatomy of a College Degree" and found that: "...Elementary teachers take fewer hours in English and mathematics combined than they do in social sciences. Yet the first two are the areas to which they will give the greatest attention in the elementary grades....The mathematics course enrollments indicate that large numbers of college students are taking a high-school level program. If what is true in mathematics is also true in other disciplines, the freshman and sophomore years for many students do not represent 'higher' education."[13]

We are already experiencing shortages in the number of teachers adequately trained in science. According to the National Science Teachers Association, only a quarter of those who teach science at the elementary level took 12 or more hours of science courses in college.[14] In a study conducted for the National Commission on Excellence in Education, 50 percent of elementary school teachers reported that their undergraduate training did not prepare them to teach science.[15] At a time when we are facing what the head of the National Science Foundation's education unit

48

calls "a situation… far more critical and consequential than during the post-Sputnik era," we must insist that those who will teach science first learn it themselves.

Other elements of teachers' own preparation are in similar trouble. A startling survey recently published in the *Journal of Educational Research* reported that of 254 elementary education majors, 61 percent could not locate England on a world map. Ninety percent could not find Vietnam. The average education major in this group could only locate 3.26 of 10 countries on the map.[16] Can we really expect these students to handle geography effectively when they begin teaching?

All this points to a conclusion: the current method of training elementary school teachers should be jettisoned. I believe it soon will be.

Earlier this year, a coalition of education school deans calling itself the Holmes Group urged the elimination of undergraduate degrees in education and their replacement by rigorous academic courses to be followed by graduate work in the education specialties. "For elementary teachers," they wrote, "this degree has too often become a substitute for learning any academic subject deeply enough to teach it well. These teachers are certified to teach all things to all children. But few of them know much about anything, because they are required to know a little of everything."[17]

A few weeks later, the Carnegie Forum on Education and the Economy echoed the theme, calling for "a bachelor degree in arts and sciences as a prerequisite for the professional study of teaching."[18]

It seems to me that, although no one specific preparatory route ought to be required for entry into the classroom, we can demand that all who teach our children in the early grades need (a) to have a solid general education, ordinarily acquired in a college of arts and sciences and demonstrated through written and oral examination; (b) to be of sound moral character; (c) to like children and want to teach them; and (d) before moving from candidate or apprentice status into full-fledged professionalism, to demonstrate via **successful classroom performance** the ability to impart knowledge and skills to children.

One of the ironies of our day is that the education of those who will teach young children is scorned by those who do advanced study and teaching in other fields. Writing in *Daedalus*, David Hawkins of the University of Colorado explains how the problem manifests itself in math and science, an area of particular concern in elementary teacher training:

> Future teachers are typically required to complete one or two courses, of which the content is regarded as so elementary as to be beneath the dignity of college lecturers; still formal in style, they are thin in content. Often those who teach such courses are themselves unfamiliar with the elementary riches of their own subject matter….[19]

In discussing the question of teachers' "methods" training, Stanford Professor Lee Shulman observes that "the sharp distinction between knowledge and pedagogy does not represent a tradition dating back centuries but, rather, is a more recent development."[20] He contends — and I agree — that the best way to acquire the skill of teaching a certain subject is by first acquiring a deep understanding of the subject itself. Tomorrow's teachers should spend their academic time in intimate contact with literature, history, mathematics, and science. But we also need to develop a new and rigorous science of pedagogy — not the quasi-academic material now found in "methods" courses, but a discipline that will really teach potential teachers the intellectual roots of their work. A new pedagogy would deal at a profound level with the "knots" that complicate children's understanding, not with the drawing-up of lesson plans.

Teacher training does not conclude with graduation. Like any other profession, teachers must keep up with new research developments, must take time to consult with each other, to read the literature, and to refresh their intellects. Administrators at the building and district level know that inservice training must be an integral part of the teaching career, especially if today's teachers are to keep pace with an expanding curriculum. Yet a great deal of teachers' current inservice training is simply more of the same — more courses in instructional methods rather than in literature or music or science. Unfortunately, this is largely a realistic response to the incentive structure built into the profession; teachers can move up the salary scale by taking more credits in the subjects required for elementary-level teaching.

If veteran teachers are to develop the same kind of professional depth we are asking of new teachers, states and school districts must change the incentive structure of an inservice training system rooted in the past. If we know that the science education of elementary teachers is inadequate, for example, administrators should develop incentives for teachers to take more science courses. If teachers lack an understanding of history or literature, administrators might look for ways to enroll teachers in the summer institutes sponsored by the National Endowment for the Humanities, or similar programs offered by colleges and universities.

If teachers want to be recognized as professionals, their profession must offer the same opportunities for scholarly inquiry and intellectual development that characterize other fields.

Certification

We should certify teachers to ensure that they know their subject matter and can communicate it effectively. Unfortunately, most certification today is pure "credentialism." Those with enough credits can display their transcripts, perhaps take a multiple-choice test, and proceed to the front of a classroom. Certification must begin to reflect our demand for excellence, not our appreciation of parchment.

Because teacher education typically requires so many specific courses, we are losing the services of thousands of potentially gifted teachers: young people who might otherwise be able to teach for a while and then go on to other fields, and experienced older Americans who might wish to teach after completing another kind of career.

Worst of all, "paper certification" may produce teachers who really do not know how to teach. It came as a shock when 45 percent of first-year teachers flunked Virginia's on-the-job evaluation last fall [23] — yet it confirmed the wisdom of requiring new teachers to demonstrate their competence in the classroom in addition to paper-and-pencil tests.

The State of New Jersey has begun to certify candidates on a new basis. It assesses their performance in a general college curriculum; they develop their teaching abilities in intensive training courses; then they begin work under the tutelage of master teachers. The results, after nearly a full school year in operation, are very encouraging: In a survey by the New Jersey Principals and Supervisors Association, just 2 of 60 principals rated the "alternative certification" program as "less than successful."[21] Heading into its second year, the program is oversubscribed. It is expected that one quarter of all new teachers hired in the 1986 school year in New Jersey will have entered via alternative certification.

A distinction should be made, though, between the "alternative certification" approach being implemented in New Jersey and the various kinds of emergency certifications permitted in many states. More than half the states now allow "fast track" certificates of one kind or another and there is evidence that, in their desperation to fill vacancies, some school systems are hiring unqualified personnel — or asking them to teach outside their fields. A 1985 study by the American Federation of Teachers and the Council for Basic Education found massive misassignment of teachers. According to AFT president Albert Shanker, 200,000 teachers are teaching in areas for which they are not certified.[22] Writes Dan Cheever, "We risk losing gains in the overall quality of education if we merely substitute quantity for quality in the teaching profession."

CHAPTER IV:

SCHOOL POLICY

Within America's elementary schools, there exists a host of common problems related to school organization and policy. School boards, superintendents, and state legislators would do well to ponder these areas:

Standards For All Children

It may seem kindly and benevolent for educators to look the other way when they know a child is failing to master required knowledge. But passing children from grade to grade does them no favor. Rather, it is an injustice whose cost will be borne by the child.

Elementary schools are not established simply to provide protective custody for children. They are institutions of learning and they should adhere to fair but rigorous standards. From the first day of school, children and parents alike should know what achievements will be expected of them at each level. They should also know that advancement will not take place until those goals have been reached, those standards met.

> *The first requirement for a good school is that it rest on values that are good. The second requirement is that it be efficient in promoting the good values.* —1948

Tests are important means of determining whether children have acquired enough knowledge to move on, and it is essential that fair, complete, and periodic assessments take place. But testing can be overdone or misunderstood. It should not swamp the curriculum or dominate classroom time. Study Group member Lois Coit tells of one elementary school in which reading scores were lagging; rather than starting a library, which the school lacked, administrators bought the students a workbook series on how to take tests. Obviously, this was a case of assessment gone awry.

We need to understand that virtually all children can meet minimum educational standards if given the time and resources. That's why it's so wrong to expect less of them. Taking extra time to reach a standard should not mean "failing"; it should mean "succeeding"—by working a little longer. Sending children through school in chronological lockstep means that we cannot give a particular child the time needed to make the grade. We may pat ourselves on the back now, but the child "socially promoted" today will get slapped by reality tomorrow.

> *Two things are needed to enhance public faith in what the schools may be doing. One is for the public to become more familiar with the schools. The other is for their schools to have available better means to assess for themselves, and for the public, the results of the educational process.* — *1953*

As Howard Miller, former president of the Los Angeles Board of Education, says, "All too often those who suffer the most from no-fail policies are students from disadvantaged backgrounds, including minorities...."[1] His views are echoed by *Washington Post* columnist William Raspberry, who writes about the problem of black children lagging generally on standardized tests: "Outlawing tests in an effort to mask these unpleasant facts makes about as much sense as outlawing thermometers and electrocardiograph machines to mask the fact that minorities tend to suffer poorer health."[2]

The cruelest thing schools can do is to pamper non-achievers early, and then lower the boom later on, in high school proficiency exams. Elementary school must provide a firm foundation, even if it takes a little longer. As Georgetown University basketball coach John Thompson said in reference to college athletes who flunk: "It wasn't a coach who passed these kids from grades one through six when they weren't able to read."[3]

Resources

Education is not free, and good schools are not cheap. Some elementary schools plainly lack the financial resources they need. Yet as a society we invest an immense amount of money in the enterprise as a whole, and the amount keeps rising: More than $146 billion was spent on public elementary and secondary schools in 1985-86.[4] In the school year about to start, our public schools will spend an average per pupil in excess of $4,000 per year,[5] which is to say that a class of 25 youngsters will occasion a public investment greater than $100,000. That represents a 236 percent increase, adjusted for inflation, since 1950. Can anyone argue that the quality or performance of our education system has risen by a comparable figure during the same period?

Besides parents and taxpayers, other portions of the American community contribute to education. In the past several years, for example, more than 40 cities have established foundations for the support of public education, under the guidance of the Public Education Fund in Pittsburgh. By underwriting teachers' professional development and helping to defray the cost of school expenses, these foundations assist schools to improve.

In general, the American people are willing to pay for the education of our children. Yet questions of equity persist. A recent study published in the *Texas Tech Journal of Education* showed that rural teachers earn significantly less than their urban and surburban counterparts.[6] State officials should keep this problem in mind when considering strategies for attracting teachers into rural areas.

The business community has a particular stake in the education of young children. However, its attention has been directed toward levels of schooling nearer the point of hire—the high schools and colleges from which it will soon draw new employees. In 1984, according to the Council for Financial Aid to Education, 411 corporations surveyed donated $562 million to education at all levels. Yet only $26.1 million was donated to pre-college education—with most of that going to secondary schools.[7] I believe it is time for the manufacturing and service sectors to recognize the importance of elementary education in the scheme of their own interests. Business people seldom complain about prospective employees' lack of knowledge in graduate philosophy—but they are constantly surprised by applicants who cannot read or write a report in plain English. Employers should stop wondering why the workforce lacks basic skills, and start helping elementary schools deliver a better graduate.

Some farsighted business people have made it their business to work for improvement at the elementary level. One of these is Arthur Gunther, Jr., who served on the Study Group while president of Pizza Hut, Inc. That company's "Book-It" program offers grade-school children the tempting incentive of a free pizza if they read a certain number of books each month. On a visit to a first-grade class at Philadelphia's Jenks School, members of the Study Group were delighted to find every child qualifying for a free pizza! This may cost the company a few dollars in the short run but will help provide a better-educated workforce a few years from now. President Reagan recently presented Pizza Hut with a White House award for private sector initiatives—an honor richly deserved. Youngsters who start reading for a pizza will soon discover the pleasures of another and greater kind of nourishment.

Another trend in the business community is very encouraging. Eugene Lang and Charles Benenson are among the growing number of successful individuals who are earmarking a part of their own wealth for children's futures. By promising to finance the college educations of entire classes in certain hard-pressed schools, these businessmen are providing a unique incentive for children to stay in school and do well there. There are more than 400,000 millionaires in the United States today[8]— roughly five for every elementary school—and I commend to all of them the examples of Mr. Lang and company. They are superb demonstrations of how individual responsibility sustains the covenant of education.

Discipline

At the elementary level, there is little overt violence (although 6-year-olds can be pretty rambunctious). There is, however, a real necessity to promote what James Enochs, Assistant Superintendent of the Modesto, California, schools, calls "The Fourth R—Responsibility." Sociologist Amitai Etzioni, writing about "the pivotal role of self-discipline" in building an adult community, observed that: "A significant proportion of the children who enter American schools each year seem to be psychically underdeveloped. Their families have not helped them mature to the point where they can function effectively in a school, relate constructively to its rules, authorities, and 'work' discipline."[9]

> *It is, of course, understood by your committee that the substantial moral training of the school is performed by the discipline rather than by the instruction in ethical theory. The child is trained to be regular and punctual, and to restrain his desire to talk and whisper—in these things gaining self-control day by day. The essence of moral behavior is self-control.*
>
> *—1895*

Elementary teachers thus find themselves expending precious class time and personal energy simply to get order. Clearly, the largest responsibility for developing self-discipline in children rests in the home. And where a child has serious problems in controlling behavior or focussing attention, the services of other professionals within the school—counselors and school psychologists—may be of vital importance. But in more routine disciplinary issues, teachers and principals should be able to act authoritatively to preserve order. A disruptive child must not be able to deprive other children of their education or teachers of the ability to teach serious learners.

School officials who take care to lay down clear disciplinary guidelines will find parents—and the courts—behind them. While it is of course true, as the Supreme Court said in *Tinker v. Des Moines Independent School District,* that "students do not shed their constitutional rights at the schoolhouse door," court decisions have given teachers and principals sufficient latitude to deal with disruption.

Every school should have a discipline code, making clear to children and to parents what the school expects of them. Then it should enforce that code.

Drugs

Although drugs have been more of a secondary-level problem, they need to become a prime concern of elementary schools as well. A recent survey by *Weekly Reader* magazine showed that even in grades four through six, about 40 percent of the children thought drugs were the most serious problem at school—more than three times the total reported for any other problem.[10]

It is alarming that the drug scourge has touched such young lives. Teachers, principals, and parents must work together on drug-education programs. The most effective programs have these objectives for student learning: to value and maintain sound personal health; to respect laws and rules prohibiting drugs; to resist pressures to use drugs; to promote drug-free student activities that offer healthy avenues for children's interests. "Just Say No" clubs are among the most popular of these programs.

There can be no higher priority for educators than saving young minds and bodies and souls from drugs. Within the law, **schools should do whatever is necessary**

56

to rid themselves of drugs. The Department of Education will soon issue a separate report describing in some detail strategies parents and educators can follow.

Class Size

Almost everyone has a strong opinion about class size. Most teachers— and a lot of other people—think classes should be smaller. Others point to a considerable body of research over the years indicating that there is no clear relationship between smaller classes and higher pupil achievement. Some note that the average size of elementary school classes in Japan is 39 children,[11] compared with our 23,[12] yet Japanese youngsters consistently outscore Americans on international comparisons, and about 90 percent of them go on to graduate from high school.[13]

Indiana's Governor Robert Orr, a member of the Study Group, is deservedly proud of his state's PRIME TIME program, which is systematically reducing class size in the early grades of Indiana schools. But one reason PRIME TIME succeeds is that it provides inservice training for teachers so they can employ instructional techniques appropriate to the smaller classes. (For example, while lectures can be effective in conveying information to large groups, a dozen first graders may benefit more from individual conversation.)

Smaller classes sound right, especially for young children. But smaller classes alone might not be the best use of the resources required to achieve them. Perhaps more good can be done by providing the teacher of a large class with an aide, a specialist of some kind, a bevy of volunteer tutors, or a set of computers. Perhaps the school as a whole would be better off if it added a library, a gym program, a science specialist or a music teacher. Perhaps the crux of the problem the teacher faces is not absolute numbers of children but, rather, 2 or 3 "problem kids" in a class of 28 or 32, a problem that might well be solved in quite a different way. Maybe the children in the school would get greater mileage from an after-school enrichment program or a "Saturday school." If resources are available, maybe it would be a wiser investment simply to increase the salaries of the best of the regular teachers.

In short, let's not take for granted that smaller classes are a panacea for elementary education. At the same time, let's recognize that the teacher facing 30 kids all day, without a breather and without another adult anywhere in sight, might legitimately conclude that life would be more pleasant—and instruction more effective—if there were only 18 children in the room.

Parents And Preschool

Sometime between infancy and first grade, parents have to make the first big decision about their children's schooling: Should the child be enrolled in some sort of preschool? Of course, preschools differ considerably in their educational philosophies, sponsorship, structure, and methods. Making the right choices can be perplexing: Preschools are not interchangeable and some parents will want to   57 get expert help. Those who determine educational policy should consider ways of clarifying the options for parents of very young children.

Parents facing these decisions should bear in mind, first of all, that their children may not be **ready** for formal learning. As Study Group member Jean Marzollo put it: "Parents must understand that we can do our children harm by pushing them.... As parents, we can give our children good nutrition, but we can't make their teeth come in. Good educational nutrition means talking with children, listening to them, reading picture books to them, sharing pride in their discoveries and giving them lots of love."

When children are ready for instruction, a great deal depends on the imagination and concern which educators bring to their task. Montaigne reminded us: "Children's plays are not sports, and should be regarded as their most serious actions." The Ivy Leaf School in Philadelphia, whose principal, Liller Green, is a member of the Study Group, encourages small children to begin acquiring the skills that lead to reading. A visitor to Ivy Leaf's preschool classes can see children as young as 2½ years playing "alphabet bingo" and beginning to put sounds together. These are not exceptional children, but they are in an exceptional setting. Instruction is delivered in an atmosphere of warmth and concern.

In the same way, many parents foster early interest in sounds and letters with alphabet books and magnetic letters on the refrigerator. The idea is not to rush children into reading, but to enjoy all the preparatory steps that lead up to it, much as we enjoy children's earliest efforts at speech for a long time before we expect them to utter grammatical sentences in perfect English.

Many people are pondering the mixed merits of universal schooling for 4-year-olds. New York City has recently adopted a pilot project aimed at making public education available—though not necessarily in school settings—to all children at 4 years of age. Yet there are legitimate questions as to whether other systems should automatically follow suit. New York's experiment is designed to serve a population of 100,000 children, of whom 60 percent are near or below the poverty line. A substantial number belong to language-minority groups.

Thousands of middle-class parents also opt for preschool programs; New York's Commission on Early Childhood Education notes that 63 percent of families with annual incomes over $20,000 already enroll their children in preschool programs. But, as the Commission concedes, little research has been done on the effect of such programs on middle-class children.[14]

The essential point about preschool education is that no one prescription is right for all families. Programs will and should vary greatly in the philosophies by which they operate, the needs they meet, and the manner in which they are run. Sponsors, too, should be varied, as indeed they are today. As child psychologist David Elkind recently pointed out: "Consider the children of working parents. Only 15 percent of such parents send their children to nursery school or to day-care centers. Forty percent of these children are cared for in some other person's home, and another

31 percent are cared for by someone within the parents' own home."[15]

From the retired nurse who looks after a few children in her own apartment, to the church that organizes a three-morning-a-week nursery school for the littlest progeny of its congregants, to the day-care center attached to the parents' workplace, to the large-scale 4-year-olds' program undertaken by a public-school system—a world of choices is now emerging. Parents' decisions should be guided by their children's needs, not by the mere availability of this or that program. A child fortunate enough to have a parent or other caring adult at home, in a setting providing intellectual stimulation and socializing experiences, is likely well off without formal school, at least until kindergarten. Yet children whose home life is spent parked in front of the television set, or hanging out on the sidewalk, may find a better environment in a structured preschool.

Kindergarten

Some of these issues linger into kindergarten. Should it be mainly a place for creative play, or formal instruction, or both? According to a survey by Educational Research Service, 62.6 percent of kindergarten programs focus primarily on academic and social preparation for first grade. 49.6 percent of school districts list policies for teaching reading in kindergarten "for those ready and able." Only 11.2 percent of elementary school principals answered "none or low" when asked where academics rank among their priorities for kindergarteners.[16] Study Group member Lauren Resnick says: "I don't think kindergarten is an ambiguous issue anymore. It's school and it's here to stay."

Within our Study Group there was ambivalence about the purposes of kindergarten. Jean Marzollo, for example, cautioned against turning it into "boot camp" for first grade. "Kindergarten should have its own intellectually challenging, age-appropriate program," she says, "just as every other grade should. We know that young children learn best from concrete experiences and play. Some children are ready to move from the concrete to the abstract earlier than others—the ability to read signals such a move. Programs must be flexible enough to handle individual differences."

Let us bear in mind that children are not mini-professors or pint-sized executives. Cautions Study Group member Lois Coit: "Some parents may simply be making their children do too much, using up a child's energy and time on adjusting to new situations. A child who goes from nursery school to a play group to dance class all in one day may be too busy."

By whatever path her charges arrive at the schoolroom door, a first grade teacher should expect to receive in September a class of boys and girls ready to be intimately acquainted with the 3 R's. But we may be better off building in a "pre-first" grade transition year for some youngsters, and sending them to first grade when they are 7, rather than assuming that every child's greatest need is for organized, 59 cognitive learning at 5. Again, this is apt to be a judgment better made by parents and teachers than by distant policymakers and administrators.

Special Education

Since the passage of Public Law 94-142 in 1975, this nation has viewed as a solemn obligation the education of all children— including those with learning problems. Yet it has proved difficult to translate legal commitments and good intentions into workable everyday arrangements.

"Learning disability" is a broad term which may apply to very different conditions. Some 1.8 million children were classified as "learning disabled" during the 1984-85 school year, and were placed in special education programs.[17] Still another 10 to 20 percent of the school population may experience learning or behavior problems that hinder their progress. For educators, a slow learner presents quite different challenges from those of a very bright child who is dyslexic.

Since our arrangement of grades presumes that children learn at roughly the same rate, those with learning problems of any sort must be dealt with as exceptions. PL 94-142 requires that they be educated in the "least restrictive environment"— that is, in an educational setting as close as possible to the regular classroom; but some districts discourage schools from providing those services in the regular class. Thus, many students who are educable in normal classroom settings wind up in "pullout" classes, where education may become fractured and compartmentalized. They are better served, in most cases, by schools that can provide a continuum of educational experiences.

More than other children, those with learning problems require individual attention. Yet many of today's schools are unable to give it. Teachers who are asked to provide such instruction may not be sufficiently trained in the appropriate techniques; principals may have had no training at all in this area. (Only seven states now require administrators to have had preparation in the education of handicapped children as part of their teaching or administrative certificate.[18]) And state or local regulations may interfere with the school's ability to make autonomous decisions about how best to serve its students. For example, a state education agency may limit the number of students to be served by an itinerant special education teacher— although that teacher may be quite capable of handling more.

Schools also face the problem of appropriate evaluation. Children may be labelled "learning disabled" simply because they score low on a standardized test, because they present conventional behavior problems that confound the classroom teacher, or because a school will only receive state or Federal funds if the child can be counted as part of a special program. The population known as "learning disabled" has more than doubled since 1976, due in part to such evaluation problems.

It should be made clear that not all children who lag in reading, or who fail to excel on standardized tests, have a clinical disorder. School administrators should tailor remedial activities to the specific problem; special education must not be used as a dumping ground for other difficulties.

In *Becoming a Nation of Readers*, for example, Jeanne Chall estimates that up to one-third of Americans have serious reading difficulties. She notes: "This group includes children from low-income families, ethnic minorities, non-English or recent speakers of English, and those with specific reading and learning disabilities." Special education classes are appropriate only for the last of these groups. Decisions to recommend such classes must involve teachers, parents and school counselors, whose combined familiarity with the child may add up to a better diagnosis than one arrived at by any one party acting alone.

The Gifted Child

A recent study by the Sid W. Richardson Foundation asserted: "The way America educates its brightest students must change. Public schools reward behavior inappropriate for an independent thinker, researcher, or artist."[19] Too often today, the education of gifted children is fragmented in the same ways as is special education — administered in pullout classes that provide enrichment in specialized settings.

Study group member Diane Ravitch makes the crucial point: What we now teach **some** children in "gifted and talented" programs was once part of the standard curriculum for average children in ordinary classes. Our largest challenge in elementary education is to establish once again a situation in which **every** youngster gets a full measure of literature, history, languages, science, math, and writing. Were we to do that, uncommonly able boys and girls would simply move at a faster pace through the regular curriculum, perhaps completing elementary school sooner, perhaps spending seventh and eighth grade in a special program, perhaps just getting deeper into things through independent projects, additional reading, extra assignments, and more library work. Breaking the chronological lockstep of age-grading would likely turn out to be a boon for slow learners as well as able students.

> *In all good school systems the pupils take up new work when they have completed the old, and the bright pupils are transferred to higher classes when they have so far distanced their fellows that the amount of work fixed for the average ability of the class does not give them enough to do.* —1895

But special opportunities may also need to be furnished. Provided that the principles of school diversity and parent choices are accepted, it may follow naturally that schools stressing a classical curriculum, or math and science, will serve as magnets for gifted boys and girls. Let us not overlook the value of special accelerated summer programs, of weekend and after-school programs, and of enrichment programs run by institutions other than schools, including libraries, museums, colleges, and churches. Highly talented children are resources that no society can afford to waste.

61

Textbooks

Who decides what gets taught in elementary schools? According to Dan Cheever, "vast swaths of the curriculum are determined by publishers' views of what will sell to state and local school boards, by local school boards' views of what 'back-to-basics' means to parents, and by teachers' views of what they are told to do by everyone else."

Yes, the availability of textbooks influences what is taught—and how it is taught. But the curricular requirements of states and localities influence the textbooks, too. Textbook publishing is market-responsive. The publishers will sell what their customers insist on buying. The fundamental responsibility for setting publishers' guidelines rests with state and local school policymakers and administrators, influenced—though rarely enough—by teachers and parents.

Policymakers do not always perform this task wisely, yet publishers still have to respond. Consider the phenomenon known as "mentioning." In order to comply with states' curricular frameworks, publishers may have to cram thousands of facts into language arts or social studies textbooks, no matter what the consequences for literary style and meaning. The result, says analyst Harriet Tyson-Bernstein, is that textbooks get turned into "a dumping ground for facts"—not a tool for learning.[20]

Language-Minority Children

Jo Gusman, a member of the Study Group, teaches second and third grades at the Newcomer School in Sacramento, California. Her own experience in the classroom vividly illustrates the changing nature of elementary-school populations. Children at the Newcomer School arrive speaking 27 different languages, and Gusman must find a way of communicating effectively with students who speak Farsi or Vietnamese or Creole. While the Newcomer School is a dramatic example, many of our elementary schools are welcoming refugees from many lands.

At the same time, America's Hispanic and Asian-American minorities are growing, and schools in virtually every large city must determine how best to educate children for whom Spanish or an Indochinese language is the first language.

Every community is different. No one policy can accommodate all the needs of language-minority children across the United States. Some come from families who encourage their acquisition of English; some run in peer groups where the native language is a matter of pride. Some arrive speaking languages from which the transition to English is relatively easy; others speak languages whose entire structure is perplexingly different from ours. I believe that two guidelines ought to pertain in all cases:

a) All American children have a right to an excellent education; and

b) All American children need to learn to speak, read, and write English as soon as possible.

Beyond that, the specific methodology should be a matter for local decision.

CHAPTER V:

IN THE SCHOOLS

The Future Is Here...

Of the 847 students at the Futures Academy in Buffalo, New York, nearly 80 percent come from low-income families. This is a public magnet school, developed in response to a court's desegregation order—and it has put together a unique program that responds to the realities of the surrounding area. Unemployment is a substantial problem in Buffalo, and as the school's staff understands, the children need to sense that their education will be worth something after graduation. So the school has set up business partnerships and a "career awareness" program. Students take "mini-courses" in Tourism, Banking, Hotels, and other fields. They actually get to spend some time working at their occupations. Civics takes on real forms as well: Students conduct trials and hold class and "town" elections.

The instructional program is demanding—carefully paced and sequenced. Discipline is not much of a problem; not only do children and their parents sign a "contract" laying out what is expected of them, the students are simply too busy to get into much trouble. The school band has played on the Capitol steps in Washington; children participate in Buffalo's Ethnic Festival; they have done science projects for a museum competition; and there is a full array of sports—from volleyball to ski outings.

Standardized tests don't measure all the enthusiasm and life at the Futures Academy, but they certainly tell a story of booming academic achievement. The percentage of third-graders at or above grade level in math jumped from 65 percent in 1982-83 to 92 percent in 1984-85. Third graders reading at or above grade level zoomed from 58 to 87 percent in the same period. The future looks bright at the Futures Academy.

A Garden Of Many Hues...

Garden Gate Elementary, in Cupertino, California, is a harbinger of things to come—a school whose enrollment reflects the increasing ethnic diversity of our country. Its student body is 30 percent Asian, 8 percent Hispanic, 3 percent black, and   63

59 percent white—and in a district with only 3 percent low-income families, about 25 percent of Garden Gate's students are from disadvantaged families, many of them headed by single parents. Thirteen percent of the students are enrolled in special education programs.

Somehow, Garden Gate manages to take all these elements and mix them into a bubbling cauldron of instructional creativity. Education is "hands-on" at this school. The science materials are old—but the sixth graders have planted a forest in a nearby vacant lot. The library needs to be upgraded, but the children really **read** what is in it, because the school provides quiet reading time after lunch. There is a high level of parent involvement: The PTA members learned sign language in order to help with special-ed children, and many children sport clothing knitted for them by members of the grandmothers' club. Affection, respect, and recognition are two-way streets at Garden Gate. Each week, there are special assemblies where the children can give awards to any adult. At the beginning of the school year, every teacher gets a gift of $100 from the PTA—no strings attached. The teachers understand that they are appreciated by the school and the community.

Garden Gate Elementary seems to understand that excellence grows from dedication and respect—and a little fun, too.

A School on Task

Johnson Elementary in Bridgeport, West Virginia, has put into practice a body of research on "effective schools." High expectations are set, and the school is organized to promote serious learning. Acquisition of basic skills has the highest priority, and the friendly atmosphere helps children to reach their potential. Homework is an integral part of the curriculum. It is never given out as punishment or "busy work," and it is usually begun in class under teacher supervision. Since volunteers handle much of the clerical work, teachers can concentrate on teaching. "Time on task" is stressed.

The community surrounding Johnson is generally affluent—but the school must also accommodate scores of disadvantaged and transient students. Its program ranges from remediation to enrichment, making all the stops in between. By stressing academic excellence, Johnson Elementary succeeds: 90 percent of its students read at or above grade level, and **99 percent** are at or above grade level in math.

This is a school where thoughtful organization helps children excel.

"They Teach You To Succeed"

Caloosa Elementary in Cape Coral, Florida, is one of those schools where one strength reinforces another. It provides a host of school-wide activities that allow children to take their classroom knowledge and apply it across the boundaries of academic disciplines. There's a Young Authors Contest, a Science Fair, a Cultural

Fair, and a wealth of activities showing how knowledge gets applied in real life. These range from a post office to a bank, from a school store to a publishing company.

How does the whole thing run? Principal Mary Santini sees that her teachers have numerous opportunities to consult, to review programs in other schools, and to grow in their own knowledge. Teachers work "across disciplines" in order to learn what information students lack. They do team teaching. Recently, one class wrote books during English class and then bound them in art class. There is a special emphasis on drawing material from various subjects in order to build critical thinking and independent reasoning. Caloosa has shown a steady improvement in test scores over the past few years, and students love the place. They told one visitor that Caloosa is a 'great school' because "they teach you to succeed."

These are just a few glimpses of what is possible in America's elementary schools. We know excellence is possible because we can see it today in many places. Excellence is not manufactured in Washington; it does not get mandated by state legislatures or appropriated by city councils. It begins with individual schools and people—with parents who demand and then play a significant role in their children's education; with principals who have a clear vision and who know how to lead their schools; with teachers dedicated to advancing knowledge and free to do their professional work.

Excellence is found in the most affluent suburbs and in the midst of oppressive poverty. While adopting measures to lift the general level of America's elementary schools and paying special attention to those who need help the most, we should keep in mind that excellence can be achieved anywhere.

That it is already being achieved—and can be seen—is evidence that elementary education in the United States is not a disaster area. It is not, so far as I and members of the Study Group can determine, threatened by a rising tide of mediocrity. On the contrary, it's pretty good right now. But outstanding examples are too few, satisfactory institutions are not numerous enough, and the norm or average is not high enough. Overall, elementary education in the United States can and must improve if it is to provide a strong enough foundation for all that we need to construct atop it. It is within our capacity as a society to complete that foundation. I believe we have got the will and the imagination, that we are prepared to continue devoting the resources, and that we possess the necessary knowledge and ideas. Improving a large, decentralized enterprise is never a simple or speedy undertaking. But if our communities demand excellence as a goal in their elementary schools, and if principals and teachers are given the necessary resources and professional autonomy, excellence will result.

I am not so worried about the schools themselves as about the broader condition of elementary education, defined—at the outset—as "everything that children learn, for good or for ill, before adolescence." Will the community of adults shoulder its weighty and diverse responsibilities toward the children who will be our new adults at the beginning of the 21st century? Or will we—all of us—pause briefly and then return to our customary pursuits, consigning children once again to the attention of others?

The 31 million American children who return to elementary school this fall have a lot riding on our decisions.

Members Of The Elementary Education Study Group

Jeanne S. Chall
Professor of Education
Director of the Reading Laboratory
Harvard University
Cambridge, Massachusetts

Daniel S. Cheever, Jr.
President
Wheelock College
Boston, Massachusetts

Lois Coit
Journalist
Lexington, Massachusetts

John Curnutte
Assistant Professor of Pediatrics
University of Michigan
Ann Arbor, Michigan

Charles Glenn
Director, Bureau of Equal Educational Opportunity
Commonwealth of Massachusetts
Quincy, Massachusetts

Cecil Good
Executive Director, Instructional Technology
Detroit, Michigan, Schools

Liller Green
Founder and Principal
Ivy Leaf School
Philadelphia, Pennsylvania

Arthur Gunther
President and Chief Executive Officer
La Petite Boulangerie, Inc.
Mill Valley, California

Jo Gusman
Teacher, Grades 2-3
Newcomer School
Sacramento, California

Michael S. Joyce
Executive Director
Bradley Foundation
Milwaukee, Wisconsin

Rita Kramer
Author
New York, New York

Leanna Landsmann
Editor-In-Chief and Publisher
Instructor Magazine
New York, New York

Hon. Anne Lindeman
State Senator
Phoenix, Arizona

Jean Marzollo
Author/School Board President
Cold Spring, New York

Edgar Nease
Senior Minister
Dilworth United Methodist Church
Charlotte, North Carolina

Hon. Robert D. Orr
Governor of Indiana
Indianapolis, Indiana

Diane Ravitch
Adjunct Professor of History and Education
Teachers College, Columbia University
68 New York, New York

Lauren Resnick
Professor of Psychology and Education
Director, Learning Research and Development Center
University of Pittsburgh
Pittsburgh, Pennsylvania

Allan Shedlin, Jr.
Executive Director
Elementary School Center
New York, New York

Donald Thomas
Deputy Superintendent for Public Accountability
State of South Carolina
Columbia, South Carolina

Elizabeth Wisley
Principal
James L. Dennis Elementary School
Oklahoma City, Oklahoma

170-868 O - 87 - 3 : QL 3

Acknowledgments

In addition to members of the Study Group, others deserve thanks for their assistance in preparing this report:

Those who made presentations before meetings of the Study Group, including Samuel G. Sava, Executive Director, National Association of Elementary School Principals; Charles Green, former Chairman, Elementary School Commission, Southern Association of Colleges and Schools; Gary Sykes of Stanford University; Emily Feistritzer, Director of the National Center for Education Information; Martha Brown, author of *Schoolwise*; Margaret Brown and Linda Alford, of the Institute for Research on Teaching, Michigan State University; Kent D. Peterson, Director of The Principals' Institute, Vanderbilt University; Bruce Cooper of Fordham University; Herbert Walberg of the University of Illinois; Robert Hogan of the University of Tulsa; and Dorothy Rich, President of the Home and School Institute. Their work contributed immeasurably to the creation of this report, and I appreciate their generosity in sharing it with us.

In writing this report, I was fortunate to have the counsel of many colleagues within and outside the Department of Education. Among those who reviewed drafts and assisted in research, several deserve particular thanks: Chester E. Finn, Jr., Assistant Secretary for Educational Research and Improvement and Counselor to the Secretary; William Kristol, Chief of Staff; Milton Goldberg, Director, Programs for the Improvement of Practice; Nelson Smith, Staff Director of the Elementary Education Study Group; Lynn Spencer of the Office of Educational Research and Improvement; and Neal Kozodoy.

Finally, I want to thank the many Americans who took the time to help, in one fashion or another, during this inquiry: the teachers who responded to the *Instructor* Magazine survey; the members of the various organizations and societies who shared their views on elementary education; and hundreds of citizens who wrote, called, and otherwise communicated their thoughts about the education of our young children.

Footnotes

Introduction

1. National Center for Health Statistics, *Monthly Vital Statistics, "Advance Report of Final Natality Statistics, 1983,"* volume 34 number 6, Supplement, September 20, 1985; and 1984-86 estimates by the U.S. Bureau of the Census.
2. Unpublished data from the U.S. Department of Education, Center for Statistics.
3. The last major national report on elementary education was *Elementary School Objectives*, The Russell Sage Foundation, 1953.
4. Address, National Press Club, March 27, 1985.

Chapter I

1. U.S. Department of Education, Center for Statistics.
2. Hodgkinson, Harold L., "All One System," Institute for Educational Leadership, Inc., 1985.
3. Seabrook, Luther, *Five Steps to Excellence*, Superintendent's Report, Community School District V, New York City, New York, 1986.
4. U.S. Department of Health and Human Services, National Center for Health Statistics, *National Estimates of Marriage Dissolution and Survivorship: United States*, Series 3, Number 19, November 1980.
5. U.S. Department of Labor, *Bureau of Statistics News Release*, USOL 85-381, September 1985.
6. U.S. Bureau of the Census, *Statistical Abstract of the United States*, 106th edition, 1986.
7. Levine, Ken, "Some Parents Don't Bother," *Baltimore Evening Sun*, November 20, 1985.
8. National Rural Research and Personnel Preparation Project (NRP), *Effective Service Delivery Strategies Appropriate for Specific Rural Subcultures*, National Rural Development Institute, Bellingham, Washington, December 1980.

9. Stevenson, Harold W., "Mathematics Achievement of Chinese, Japanese and American Children," *Science*, February 14, 1986.

10. See the 1981 to 1985 *Neilsen Report*, A.C. Neilsen Company, Northbrook, Illinois.

11. Strasburger, Victor C., M.D.: "When Parents Ask About the Influence of TV on Their Kids," *Contemporary Pediatrics*, May 1985.

12. Morrow, Lance, "Have We Abandoned Excellence?" *Time Magazine*, March 22, 1982.

13. U.S. Bureau of the Census, Current Population Report, Series P20, Number 398, *Household and Family Characteristics: March 1984.*

14. Long, Thomas J. and Lynette Long, *Latchkey Children*, Washington. D.C., National Institute of Education, 1983. ERIC Document No. ED 226836.

15. Reported in "When School's Out and Nobody's Home," National Committee for the Prevention of Child Abuse, 1985.

16. Tocqueville, Alexis de, *Democracy in America*, 1835.

Chapter II

1. Congressional Budget Office, *Trends in Educational Achievement*, April 1986.

2. National Assessment of Educational Progress. *The Reading Report Card: Progress Toward Excellence in Our Schools* (Report No: 15-R-01), Princeton, New Jersey: National Assessment of Educational Progress, 1985.

3. Jacobson, Willard J., and Rodney L. Doran, "The Second International Science Study: U.S. Results," *Phi Delta Kappan*, February 1985.

4. Lerner, Barbara, "American Education: How Are We Doing?" *The Public Interest*, Fall 1982.

5. Walter Lippmann, address before the American Association for the Advancement of Science, September 30, 1940.

6. Commission on Reading: *Becoming a Nation of Readers*, The National Academy of Education, The National Institute of Education and The Center for the Study of Reading, Washington, D.C., 1985.

7. National Assessment of Educational Progress, op. cit.

8. Ibid.

9. Commission on Reading, op.cit.

10. Ibid.

11. Ibid.

12. Ibid.

13. Dishaw, M., *Descriptions of Allocated Time to Content Areas for the A-B Period*, Far West Regional Laboratory for Educational Research and Development, San Francisco, California, 1977.

14. Fisher, C.W., D. Berliner, N. Filby, R. Marliave, L. Cohen, M. Dishaw, and J. Moore, *Teaching and Learning in Elementary Schools: A Summary of the Beginning Teacher Evaluation Study*, Far West Regional Laboratory, San Francisco, California, 1978.

15. Fielding, Wilson, and P.T. Anderson, "A new focus on free reading: The role of trade books in reading instruction," in T.E. Raphael and R. Reynolds (Eds.), *Contexts of Literacy*, Longman, New York, (in press).

16. Quoted in "A Debate over 'Dumbing Down,'" *Time Magazine*, December 3, 1984.

17. National Assessment of Educational Progress, *Writing Trends Across the Decade 1974-84*, Princeton, New Jersey, April 1986.

18. Bereiter, C. and M. Scarmadalia, excerpts from *The Psychology of Written Composition*, Erlbaum, Hillsdale, New Jersey (in press).

19. From the International Association for the Evaluation of Education Achievement, *Perceptions of the Intended and Implemented Mathematics Curriculum*, Second Mathematics Study, June 1985.

20. Stevenson, Harold, op. cit.

21. Cawelti, Gordon, and Janice Adkisson, "ASCD Study Reveals Elementary School Time Allocations for Subject Areas; Other Trends Noted," *Curriculum Update*, Association for Supervision and Curriculum Development, April 1985.

22. Savage, David G., "U.S. Students Top Only Third World in Math," *Los Angeles Times*, March 11, 1986.

23. Interview with Department of Education staff.

24. Bell, Max, et al., University of Chicago School Mathematics Project, *Everyday Mathematics*, Preliminary Edition, Chicago, Illinois, 1986.

25. International Association for the Evaluation of Education Achievement, op. cit.

26. "Some New Measures of Scientific Illiteracy," a paper presented by Jon D. Miller, Northern Illinois University, at the Annual Meeting of the American Association for the Advancement of Science, Philadelphia, Pennsylvania, May 28, 1986.

27. Smith, Herbert A., "A Report on the Implications for the Science Community of Three NSF-Supported Studies of the State of Precollege, Science Education," in *What are the Needs in Precollege Science, Mathematics, and Social Science Education? Views from the Field*, National Science Foundation, SE 80-9, 1980, p. 166.

28. Cawelti and Adkisson, op. cit.

29. *The Science Education Databook, 1980*: reported in "Why Kids Don't Like Social Studies," *Social Education*, May 1984.

30. Hoff-Wilson, Joan, Executive Secretary, Organization of American Historians, letter, May 13, 1986.

31. Austin, Linda and Dale Rice, "U.S. Last in Math, Low in Science on New Test," *Dallas Times Herald*, December 11, 1983.

32. Kopec, Richard J., "GEOGRAPHY: No 'Where' in North Carolina 1984," unpublished paper, University of North Carolina, Chapel Hill, 1984.

33. Harry S Truman, letter to Edward F. McFaddin, September 9, 1958, in *Off the Record*, edited by Robert H. Ferrell, 1980.

34. Thernstrom, Stephan, "The Humanities and Our Cultural Heritage,"

Challenges to the Humanities, C. Finn, D. Ravitch, and P.H. Roberts, (Eds.), Holmes and Meier, New York, 1985.

35. Brown, J. Carter, "Excellence and the Problem of Visual Literacy," *Design for Arts in Education*, November/December 1983.

36. Council of Chief State School Officers, "Arts, Education and the States: A Survey of State Education Policies," September 1985.

37. Hardiman, George, and Andra Johnson, "The Condition of Art Education," *Art Education*, volume 36, number 1, January 1983.

38. Fowler, Charles, *Report of the Task Force for Fine Arts of the Baltimore City Public Schools*, January 1986.

39. Eisner, Elliot W., "Why Art in Education and Why Art Education," *Beyond Creating: The Place for Art in America's Schools*, The J. Paul Getty Trust, 1985.

40. *President's Council on Physical Fitness and Sports, 1985 School Population Fitness Survey*, March 1986.

41. George Allen, President's Council on Physical Fitness, quoted in Dave Anderson, "This, Too, is Sports," *New York Times*, May 17, 1986.

42. See, among others, D. A. Bailey, "The Growing Child and the Need for Physical Activity," *Child in Sport and Physical Activity*, University Park Press, Baltimore, ed. by J.G. Albinson and G.M. Andrew, 1976.

43. Walberg, Herbert J., David B. Connell, Ralph R. Turner, and Larry K. Olsen, "Health Knowledge and Attitudes Change Before Behavior, A National Evaluation of Health Programs Finds," *Curriculum Update*, Association for Supervision and Curriculum Development, June 1986.

44. "From Drill Sergeant to Intellectual Assistant: Computers in the Schools," in *Carnegie Quarterly*, Volume XXX, Number 3 & 4, Summer/Fall 1985.

45. Kirk, Russell, "Can Virtue Be Taught?" Heritage Lecture, Washington, D.C., April 29, 1982.

46. Chall, Jeanne, *Learning to Read: The Great Debate*, McGraw-Hill Book Company, New York, 1967, updated 1983.

47. Stevenson, Harold W., "Classroom Behavior and Achievement of Japanese, Chinese and American Children," *Advances in Instructional Psychology*, Erlbaum, Hillsdale, New Jersey, in press.

48. Rohlen, Thomas P., "Japanese Education: If They Can Do It, Should We?" *The American Scholar*, Volume 55 Number 1, Winter 1985-86.

49. Hermansen, Kenneth L., and James R. Gove, *The Year Round School*, Linnet Books, Hamden, Connecticut, 1971.

50. Gottschalk, Earl C., "Cities Turn to Year-Round Schools as Answer to Crowded Conditions," *Wall Street Journal*, January 8, 1986.

51. Bone, John, Memorandum, Update of the Westridge Elementary School Year-Round Program, November 4, 1985.

52. Irving, R. Mac, "Many Benefits Exist For Year-round Schools," *School Board News*, June 25, 1986.

53. Ballinger, Charles, Address to the National Council on Year-Round Education Annual Executive Directors' Meeting, Anaheim, California, January 1981.

Chapter III

1. Quoted in Davidson, Jean and Casey Banas, "The Haves, the Have-nots," *The Chicago Tribune*, May 6, 1986.
2. National Association of Elementary School Principals, *Proficiencies for Principals, Kindergarten through Eighth Grade*, 1986.
3. Cooper, Bruce S., and William Lowe Boyd, The Evolution of Training for School Administrators, *Approaches to Administrative Training in Education*, J. Murphy and P. Hallinger, (Eds.), SUNY Press, Albany, New York, in press.
4. Peterson, Kent D., Comments before Elementary Education Study Group, February 11, 1986.
5. Peterson, Kent D., and Chester E. Finn, Jr., "Principals, Superintendents, and the Administrator's Art," *The Public Interest*, Number 79, Spring 1985.
6. *Effective School Principals*, A Report to the Southern Regional Education Board by Its Commission for Educational Quality, Atlanta, Georgia, 1986.
7. *Administrative Information Report*, by the National Association of Secondary School Principals and the Educational Research Service, February 1986.
8. Feistritzer, Emily, *Profile of Teachers in the United States*, National Center for Education Information, 1986.
9. Provenzo, Eugene, Robert Kottkamp, and Marilyn Cohn, "Stability and Change in a Profession: Two Decades of Teacher Attitudes, 1964-84," *Phi Delta Kappan*, April 1986.
10. Estimate in Release Accompanying American Federation of Teachers report, *Salary Trends 1986: Survey and Analysis*, June 1986.
11. *Instructor Magazine*, "Here's What You Care About Most!" May 1986.
12. Dossey, John, "The Current Status of Preservice Elementary Teacher Education Programs," *Arithmetic Teacher*, September 1981.
13. Southern Regional Education Board, *Teacher Preparation: The Anatomy of a College Degree*, Atlanta, Georgia, 1985.
14. Aldridge, William G., Executive Director, National Science Teachers Association, quoted in "Finding Answers to the Science Teaching Crisis," *New York Times*, April 6, 1986.
15. Hurd, Paul DeHart, "An Overview of Science Education in the United States and Selected Foreign Countries," paper prepared for the National Commission on Excellence in Education, 1982.
16. Herman, Wayne L., Jr., Michael Hawkins, and Charles Berryman, "World Place Name Location Skills of Elementary Pre-service Teachers," *Journal of Educational Research*, September/October 1985.
17. The Holmes Group, Inc., *Tomorrow's Teachers: A Report of the Holmes Group*, East Lansing, Michigan, April 1986.
18. Carnegie Forum on Education and the Economy, *A Nation Prepared: Teachers for the 21st Century*, The Report of the Task Force on Teaching as a Profession, May 1986.
19. Hawkins, David, "Nature Closely Observed," *Daedalus*, Spring 1983.

20. Shulman, Lee S., "Those Who Understand: Knowledge Growth in Teaching," *Educational Researcher*, February 1986.
21. Friendly, Jonathan, "Jersey's Alternative-Route Teachers Deciding Whether to Continue," *New York Times*, May 14, 1986.
22. Shanker, Albert, comments on "Making Do in the Classroom: A Report on Misassignment of Teachers," American Federation of Teachers, quoted in AFT release, September 24, 1985.
23. Reported in the *Washington Post*, D'Vera Cohn, "45% of New Teachers Tested Flunk Virginia Evaluations," April 10, 1986.

Chapter IV

1. Miller, Howard, letter to the editor, "No 'F' Grades for Youngsters," *Los Angeles Times*, March 23, 1986.
2. Raspberry, William, "Fools, Skills and Standardized Tests," *The Washington Post*, December 30, 1985.
3. Thompson, John, "Quotelines," *USA Today*, February 21, 1986.
4. U.S. Department of Education, *Digest of Education Statistics*, 1985-86; and unpublished data.
5. Ibid.
6. Barker, Bruce O., "Teachers' Salaries in Rural America," *Texas Tech Journal of Education*, Fall 1985.
7. Council for Financial Aid to Education, *Corporate Support of Education 1984*, New York, New York.
8. U.S. Bureau of the Census, *Statistical Abstract of the United States*, op. cit.
9. Etzioni, Amitai, *Self-Discipline, Schools and the Business Community*, National Chamber Foundation, Washington, D.C., 1984.
10. *The Weekly Reader National Survey on Education*, Terry Borton, Editor, Middletown, Connecticut, March 31, 1986.
11. Stevenson, Harold W., "Classroom Behavior and Achievement of Japanese, Chinese, and American Children," op. cit.
12. National Education Association, *The Status of the American Public School Teacher* 1980-81, 1982.
13. Rohlen, op. cit.
14. Early Childhood Education Commission, Final Report: *Take A Giant Step*, New York, New York, p.22, 1986.
15. Elkind, David: "In Defense of Early Childhood Education," *Principal*, p.9, May 1986.
16. Educational Research Service: "Kindergarten Programs and Practices in Public Schools", reported in *Principal*, p. 22, May 1986.
17. U.S. Department of Education, *Annual Report to Congress on the Implementation of Education for All Handicapped Children Act*, 1986.
18. U.S. Department of Education, telephone survey of state special education directors, 1986.

19. Maeroff, Gene I., "To Be Young and Gifted—and Bored," *The New York Times*, December 22, 1985.
20. Tyson-Bernstein, Harriet, "When More Is Less: The 'Mentioning' Problem in Textbooks," *American Educator*, American Federation of Teachers, Summer 1985.

Selected Bibliography

I. *Books*

Bettelheim, Bruno, *The Uses of Enchantment,* Alfred A. Knopf, New York, 1976.

Blumberg, Arthur, and Greenfield, William, *The Effective Principalship*, Allyn and Bacon, Inc., Boston, 1980.

Brown, Martha C., *Schoolwise*, Jeremy P. Tarcher, Inc., Los Angeles, 1985.

Bunzel, John (Ed.), *Challenge to American Schools*, Oxford University Press, New York, 1985.

Chall, Jeanne, *Learning to Read: The Great Debate*, McGraw-Hill Book Company, New York, 1983.

Coles, Robert, *The Moral Life of Children*, The Atlantic Monthly Press, New York, 1986.

Finn, C., Ravitch, D., and Roberts, P.H. (Eds.), *Challenges to the Humanities*, Holmes and Meier, New York, 1985.

Hermansen, Kenneth L., and Gove, James R., *The Year Round School*, Linnet Books, Hamden, Connecticut, 1971.

Sher, Jonathan P. (Ed.), *Education in Rural America*, Westview Press, Boulder, Colorado, 1977.

II. *Reports, Papers and Surveys*

A.C. Neilsen Company, *Neilsen Report, 1981–85*, Northbrook, Illinois.

American Federation of Teachers, *Making Do in the Classroom: A Report on Misassignment of Teachers*, 1985.

American Federation of Teachers, *Salary Trends 1986: Survey and Analysis*, June 1986.

Borton, Terry (Ed.), *The Weekly Reader Survey on Education*, Middletown, Connecticut, March 31, 1986.

California Commission On the Teaching Profession, *Who Will Teach Our Children?* November 1985.

Carnegie Forum on Education and the Economy, *A Nation Prepared: Teachers for the 21st Century*, The Report of the Task Force on Teaching as a Profession, May 1986.

Cawelti, Gordon, and Adkisson, Janice, "ASCD Study Reveals Elementary School Time Allocations for Subject Areas; Other Trends Noted", *Curriculum Update*, Association for Supervision and Curriculum Development, April 1985.

Commission on Reading, *Becoming a Nation of Readers,* The National Academy of Education, The National Institute of Education and The Center for the Study of Reading, Washington, D.C., 1985.

Congressional Budget Office, *Trends in Educational Achievement*, April 1986.

Council of Chief State School Officers, *Arts, Education and the States: A Survey of State Education Policies*, September 1985.

Association for Supervision and Curriculum Development, *Curriculum Update*, June 1986 (on Health Education).

Dallas Times Herald, "American Education, The ABCs of Failure," December 11, 1983.

Early Childhood Education Commission, Final Report: *Take A Giant Step*, New York, New York, 1986.

Enochs, James C., *The Restoration of Standards: The Modesto Plan*, Wayne State University Chapter of Phi Delta Kappa, 1979.

Feistritzer, Emily, *Profile of Teachers in the United States*, National Center for Education Information, 1986.

Hodgkinson, Harold, L., *All One System*, Institute for Educational Leadership, Inc., 1985.

Home and School Institute Inc., *The Forgotten Factor in School Success — The Family,* 1985.

Instructor Magazine: "Here's What You Care About Most!" May 1986.

International Association for the Evaluation of Education Achievement, *Perceptions of the Intended and Implemented Mathematics Curriculum*, Second Mathematics Study, June 1985.

Kearney, Nolan C., *Elementary School Objectives*, Russell Sage Foundation, New York, 1953.

Levin, Henry M., *The Educationally Disadvantaged: A National Crisis,* The State Youth Initiatives Project Working Paper #6, Public/Private Ventures, Philadelphia, Pennsylvania, July 1985.

National Assessment of Educational Progress, *The Reading Report Card: Progress Toward Excellence in Our Schools*, (Report No: 15-R-01) Princeton, New Jersey, 1985.

National Assessment of Educational Progress, *Writing Trends Across the Decade 1974–84*, Princeton, New Jersey, April 1986.

National Association of Elementary School Principals, *Proficiencies for Principals, Kindergarten through Eighth Grade*, 1986.

National Association of Elementary School Principals, *Standards for Quality Elementary Schools*, 1984.

National Commission on Excellence in Education, *A Nation At Risk*, April 1983.

National Committee for the Prevention of Child Abuse, "When School's Out and Nobody's Home," 1985.

National Council of Teachers of Mathematics, *An Agenda For Action*, 1980.

National Education Association of the United States Educational Policies Commission, *Education for All American Children*, Washington, D.C., 1948.

National Education Association Subcommittee Report to the Commission on Revision of Elementary Education, *Intelligence Tests and School Reorganization*, World Book Company, Yonkers-on-Hudson, New York, 1922.

National Educational Association of the United States, *Journal of Proceedings and Addresses*, Session of the Year 1895, St. Paul, Minnesota, 1895.

Southern Regional Education Board, *Effective School Principals*, Atlanta, Georgia, 1986.

Southern Regional Education Board, *Teacher Preparation: The Anatomy of a College Degree*, Atlanta, Georgia, 1985.

Supplementary Educational Monographs in conjunction with The School Review and The Elementary School Journal, *Report of the Commission on Length of Elementary Education*, University of Chicago, Chicago, Illinois, 1927.

Tomorrow's Teachers: A Report of the Holmes Group, East Lansing, Michigan, April 1986.

U.S. Department of Education, *Digest of Education Statistics*, 1985/86.

U.S. Department of Education, *The Condition of Education*, 1985.

U.S. Department of Education, *The Nation Responds*, May 1984.

U.S. Department of Education, *What Works*, 1986.

III. *Journal Articles*

Barker, Bruce O., "Teachers' Salaries in Rural America", *Texas Tech Journal of Education*, Fall 1985.

Bennett, William, "Lost Generation", *Policy Review*, Summer 1985.

Bennett, William J., and Delattre, Edwin J., "Moral Education in the School," *The Public Interest*, Winter 1978.

Farr, Roger, and Tulley, Michael A., "Do Adoption Committees Perpetuate Mediocre Textbooks?" *Phi Delta Kappan*, March 1985.

Herman, Wayne L., Jr., Hawkins, Michael, and Berryman, Charles: "World Place Name Location Skills of Elementary Pre-service Teachers," *Journal of Educational Research*, September/October 1985.

Hirsch, E.D., Jr., "Cultural Literacy," *The American Scholar*, Vol. 52, Spring 1983.

Hirsch, E.D., Jr., "Cultural Literacy and the Schools," *American Educator*, Vol. 9, No. 2, Summer 1985.

Hirsch, E.D., Jr., " 'Cultural Literacy' Doesn't Mean 'Core Curriculum'," *English Journal*, Vol. 74, No. 6, October 1985.

Jacobson, Willard, J., and Doran, Rodney L., "The Second International Science Study: U.S. Results," *Phi Delta Kappan*, February, 1985.

Lerner, Barbara, "American Education: How Are We Doing?" *The Public Interest*, Fall 1982.

Lindsey, Alfred J., "Consensus or Diversity? A Grave Dilemma in Schooling," *Journal of Teacher Education*, July-August 1985.

Murphy, Joseph, Hallinger, Philip, and Peterson, Kent D., "Supervising and Evaluating Principals: Lessons from Effective Districts, *Educational Leadership*, October 1985.

Peterson, Kent D., "Obstacles to Learning from Experience and Principal Training," *The Urban Review*, Spring 1986.

Peterson, Kent D., and Finn, Chester E., Jr., "Principals, Superintendents, and the Administrator's Art," *The Public Interest*, Number 79, Spring 1985.

Provenzo, Eugene, Kottkamp, Robert, and Cohn, Marilyn, "Stability and Change in a Profession: Two Decades of Teacher Attitudes, 1964–84." *Phi Delta Kappan*, April 1986.

Rohlen, Thomas P., "Japanese Education: If They Can Do It, Should We?" *The American Scholar*, Volume 55 Number 1, Winter 1985–86.

Shulman, Lee S., "Those Who Understand: Knowledge Growth in Teaching," *Educational Researcher*, February 1986.

Stevenson, Harold W., "Mathematics Achievement of Chinese, Japanese and American Children": *Science*, February 14, 1986.

Tucker, Marc, "From Drill Sergeant to Intellectual Assistant: Computers in the School," In *Carnegie Quarterly*, Volume XXX Number 3 & 4, Summer/Fall 1985.

Uhlenberg, Peter, and Eggebeen, David, "The Declining Well-being of American Adolescents," *The Public Interest*, Issue No. 82, Winter 1986.

Walberg, Herbert J., "Families As Partners in Educational Productivity," *Phi Delta Kappan*, February 1984.

Wynne, Edward A., and Walberg, Herbert J., "The Complementary Goals of Character Development and Academic Excellence," *Educational Leadership*, December 1985/January 1986.

GPO : 1987 O - 170-868 : QL 3